Copyri

No part of this book m
system, or transmitted in any form or by any means, electronic, mechanical, photocopying, recording, or otherwise, without express written permission of the publisher.

Free Resources

Along with this literature, I will be providing some resources free of charge to help assist you with your R2RSA journey. These will include:

- Financial Analysis Spreadsheet
- Agent/Contact Log
- Property Furniture List
- Example Company Let Contract
- Example Management Contract
- Example Non-Disclosure Agreement
- Links to Helpful Resources

As I have spelt any calculations and contract content out manually throughout this book, I would recommend reading the book in its entirety, and then re-visiting specific sections with the resources upon completion. Others in the industry do sell these resources, but I'm more than happy to provide them free of charge to support your development in the Rent to Rent Serviced Accommodation niche. What I will kindly request is a review of this book to help me develop my writing style in future iterations and publications. Details on how to receive the resources are presented at the end of this book.

Another request I have is to not blindly forward the resources to others, as they will have had no context or instruction on how to use them correctly. I do not want others to use these tools and make errors, potentially leading to poor decisions.

Disclaimer

The information presented within the following literature is for information only and is not to be used as a source of financial advice with respect to the content presented. The information inside and associated resources provided with in this book do not constitute financial or legal advice and should not be implemented without consulting a financial professional first.

The author does not make any guarantees or other promises as to any results that may be obtained from using the content within this literature. Do not make any investment decisions without performing your own research, due diligence and consulting with your financial advisor. To the maximum extent permitted by law, the author shall not be liable in the event any data, explanation, analysis, opinions, guidance, information or recommendations made within this book prove to be unreliable or incomplete or result in losses of any kind.

The content within this book is not, and does not, constitute as legal or investment advice. The author is providing this book and its contents on an "as is" basis. The use of any information or resources in this book is at your own risk.

Example contracts issued as additional resources are for information purposes only and should not be used for commercial use. The author/issuer shall not be responsible for any losses incurred through the use of these resources.

Acknowledgments

I want to provide a special thanks to Kieran Beach, Director of Kontrakt Property Limited. From the moment I met Kieran, approximately 13 months ago, it was obvious from the offset that we shared the same values and philosophies both in life and R2RSA. I have now worked with Kieran on various projects including the acquisition of R2RSA properties for our own portfolios and sourcing R2RSA properties for clients, where I can wholeheartedly recommend his work and ethics. I'd like to thank Kieran for checking the content of this book and offering his expertise throughout my R2RSA journey.

I would also like to thank my lifelong friend Alfie Redman, another checker of this book. Alfie has absolutely no R2RSA experience, therefore his comments were valuable to ensure my writing style and content was suitable for those with little R2RSA exposure, as this book is directed at beginners entering the space. Alfie is the type of friend that offers honest advice, rather than blowing smoke, which trust me, is incredibly useful when writing a book at his target market.

It takes a considerable amount of time out of a busy schedule to check literature on this scale, so again, thank you both for your support!

Table of Contents

Introduction 1

About me... 2

Chapter 1 – The Basics: What is R2RSA? 4

Common R2R Strategies 7

Chapter 2 - Begin your R2RSA Journey 10

Finding the Knowledge... 10
   Courses & Mentorship 10
   On the Job Training 12
The Essentials 14

Chapter 3 – Defining your Strategy.................. 19

Income Generation Methods.. 19
   Method 1 - Operating your own R2RSA properties 19
   Method 2 – Managing R2RSA properties 20
   Method 3 - Sourcing R2RSA properties for investors 22
Core Restrictions 24
   Time 24
   Capital 25
Strategy Recommendations.. 29
   Scenario One – Limited Time & Capital............................... 30
   Scenario Two – Limited Time with Disposable Capital 31
   Scenario Three – Time Rich with Limited Capital 32
   Scenario Four – Time Rich with Disposable Capital........... 34

Chapter 4 – Understanding the Risks 35

The Risk of Negative Cash Flow 35
   Negative Cashflow Mitigation 37
The Risk of Early Termination... 38

Early Termination Mitigation 39

Chapter 5 – Setting up your Business 41

Choosing a Company Name 41
Setting up your Business Bank Account 42
Becoming Compliant 43
    Property Ombudsman or Property Redress Scheme 43
    Company Insurance 45
    Information Commissioner's Office (ICO) 48
    Anti-Money Laundering 48
Understanding Local Law 49
Setting up your Business Socials, Website, and Documentation 50

Chapter 6 – Building your R2RSA Portfolio 55

The Company Let Contract 55
Property Desirability 58
    Property Quality 58
    Location 60
    What desirable serviced accommodation properties offer .. 62
    Property Type 63
    Furnishing 64
Finding R2RSA Properties 65
    Understanding Requirements 66
    The Search for Properties 68
Financial Analysis & ROI 72
Determining Nightly Rate and Occupancy Rates 84
    Contact the landlord or letting agent to enquire and view the property 88
Checking the property passes all statutory checks for R2RSA use 90
    Head Lease Compliance 90
    Mortgage Compliance 92

Overall Compliance 92
Securing the Property and Referencing 93
Signing the Contract 97
Clean, Setup and Staging the Property 98
Sourcing for Investors 100
    Finding & Qualifying Investors 101
    Protecting your Work 104
    Pricing your Investments (Sourcing Fee) 106
    Producing an Investor Pack 107
    Selling your Investment 108
Using Sourcers 111
Using Lead Generation 114
The Sourcing Process Summary 116

Chapter 7 – R2RSA Property Management .. 122

The Management Contract 124
Using a Channel Manager 125
Setting Nightly Rates 130
Payment Gateway Platform 133
Direct Bookings vs OTA Bookings 135
Finding Cleaners & Their Role 138
Property Security 142
Arranging the Property Services 146
    Council Tax 147
    Energy (Electricity & Gas) 149
    Water 150
    Broadband 151
    TV Licence 151
Emergencies and Repairs 152
Virtual Assistants 153
The Management Process Summary 156

Chapter 8 – The Future of R2RSA 164

Conclusion **181**

Introduction

This may seem like a strongly worded introduction, but the reason for me writing this book is to cut straight through the marketing hype surrounding the R2RSA (Rent to Rent Serviced Accommodation) strategy, providing a no-nonsense guide to navigating this space successfully and with integrity. The goal is that upon completion of this book, you have the knowledge needed to make informed decisions moving forward with the strategy, avoiding the mistakes that I have made throughout the past 18 months and earning additional cash flow with minimal risk in the process.

R2RSA can be a hugely beneficial strategy if deployed correctly, able to generate considerable income through property of which you do not own. However, with this being an unregulated market backed by unrealistic claims that you can generate outrageous income within a short period of time, it seems the industry could do with an honest reality check from the perspective of an intermediate R2RSA operator who has been through the trenches. I commonly come across false, or at the very least, unsustainable claims about R2RSA which I have addressed in a simple format for those who are new to the strategy and could benefit from relevant information on the contrary to the marketing hype.

This book will help you navigate towards a successful R2RSA journey, avoiding the common pitfalls, scams, and un-honest personnel which seem to litter the space. It's not all doom and gloom though, I will also share with you the strategy I am using to earn additional income through R2RSA in a fashion that mitigates risk as far as practically possible in an honest and legal manner. The book shall assess the following fundamentals:

- What Rent to Rent Serviced Accommodation is
- How to begin your R2RSA journey
- How you can increase cashflow through R2RSA and select an approach that suits you
- Understanding the risks of R2RSA and how to mitigate those through due-diligence
- Setting up your R2RSA business
- An assessment of sourcing, operating, and managing R2RSA properties
- My thoughts about the future of R2RSA

The information you acquire should be used as a sound foundation when entering the industry, allowing you to foresee pitfalls in the common practices of others, and make more informed decisions before departing with your hard-earned cash.

About me

Now you know why I'm writing this book, let me tell you a bit about me. My name is Frank Roberts. By day, I am an incorporated design engineer working full-time on the UK's railway network. I spend my days managing the design of electrical systems on multi-million-pound projects nationwide. My career in engineering has always been a core passion of mine, however, I took to property investing in my early twenties which has slowly inched its way into my life. I initially started at the bottom of the chain, by simply flipping my primary property whilst living in a building site. Whether you can even class this as property investment is debatable, but it did prompt me to investigate alternative methods of producing cash flow through unique property and other investment strategies. My career as an engineer has trained my mind to take the perspective of logic, which may become apparent through my robotic analysis throughout this book. Not that I purposefully try to suck the fun out of everything, but simply put this is a numbers game. If the numbers work, they work, if they don't, they don't, but I've found that a few more factors come into play with this strategy in particular which we'll delve into throughout later chapters.

My Rent-to-Rent Serviced Accommodation journey began 18 months ago, and I'm not ashamed to announce that I was a complete beginner. Now, at this point, you may be wondering - "why on earth would I read this book if the author only has 18 months of experience on the subject". It's a fair comment, but what I want to highlight is that this strategy is not rocket science. I learned the principles through paid mentorship and applied the knowledge, successfully sourcing properties for investors and setting up my properties under my business Studley Properties Ltd. 18 months is ample time to learn the core lessons which I feel are important to pass on to new starters as there is little guidance out there outside of expensive courses.

Another key and seemingly rare trait I possess is the ability to be open about this strategy. What I refuse to do is ignore detail i.e. sweep issues under the rug, which appears to be a significant problem with the R2RSA community; a prime tripping opportunity for the less informed. Therefore, I will do my utmost to give all the details possible to enhance your decision-making throughout this book.

If you have any questions about this book, feel free to contact me through my socials or via my email.

Facebook: @studleyproperties

Instagram: @studleyproperties.ltd

Email: frank.roberts@studleyproperties.co.uk

Chapter 1 – The Basics: What is R2RSA?

The term "Rent to Rent" or "R2R" is a well-known phrase in the property community, becoming an ever more popular strategy used by property entrepreneurs to earn a high return on investment through property with minimal upfront capital. Many see R2R as the gateway strategy into property investment, used to build funds for property or land acquisition. Although this is generally true, others have used R2R to build a very profitable business and continue to pursue the strategy, so there is no cap as to how big your R2R business can grow.

The different R2R strategies involve creating profit from someone else's properties. Using R2R strategies, you do not actually purchase a property, meaning you can say goodbye to expensive deposits, agent fees, solicitor fees, stamp duty, and the extensive waiting around for purchase completion dates. These expensive upfront costs are usually the barrier to entry for bidding property investors, making R2R an attractive alternative. In my opinion, the low barrier to entry seems to have attracted some less honest individuals who have completely butchered the strategy, pissing off masses of landlords and letting agents in the process by not paying rent, leaving properties in a poor state mid-contract and not fixing damage caused by guests. This has resulted in a somewhat bad name for those operators who run their businesses professionally with trust and transparency as core values. On the contrary, this low barrier to entry offers a significant opportunity to multiply your investment, opening doors to explore more capital-intensive strategies.

In general, rent-to-rent is a strategy that works exactly as it sounds. A property is rented from a property owner/landlord by an individual or company (acting as a rent-to-rent operator) for a monthly fee. We'll call this fee R1). The rent-to-rent operator subsequently lets that same property out to a 3rd party for a higher monthly fee. We'll call this fee R2. For this to be profitable for the rent-to-rent operator, they have to ensure that R2 is a higher number than R1. If achieved, the difference between the two will be labelled as the properties gross profit. However, the gross profit needs to be of sufficient size to also cover any operating costs, which we shall label C1, necessary to maintain the properties operation. Thus, creating a simple rule summarising net profitability for each rent-to-rent property.

$$Rent\ to\ Rent\ Net\ Profitability = R1 < R2 - C1$$

I have intentionally left off taxes and a whole host of other factors at this stage to keep things simple in this introduction. However, we'll delve deeper into exactly how to calculate a property's profitability later in this book.

A R2R operator then can be thought of as a facilitator. They rent a property from a landlord and use that property to generate sufficient income to cover the rental costs, operating costs and a profit for their business. Immediately, you might be thinking how can someone rent out the same property for a profit? Surely the property owner would let the property out for the higher rent value and maximise their profits? This question neatly brings us to the foundation of R2R, which is that R2R is a strategy where you can increase a property's total income by making that property more valuable to a single, or series of, end users. It's worth noting that within property investment a fairly linear correlation between profitability and time/effort is present, as presented in figure 1. This is not an absolute truth; however, I'm highlighting this point because R2R generally is a more time-consuming, labour-intensive, strategy compared to that of the Buy to Let strategy, which is what most landlords are deploying. By putting more time and effort into specific marketing strategies and fixing pain points by offering unique services with someone else's property, you can successfully generate more cash flow with a landlord's property than the landlord can using traditional property strategies. This is what creates the profitability margin discussed earlier.

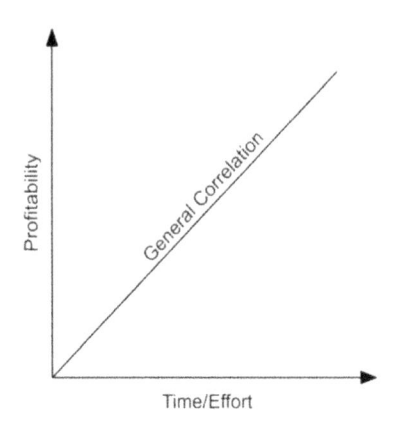

Figure 1 – General Time/Profitability Correlation

This doesn't answer the question as to why landlords don't utilise these strategies to maximise their profitability. From my experience, generally, landlords do not follow these principles for the following reasons.

- They simply don't realise they can utilise these methods to increase cash flow i.e. they are uneducated on the subject or;
- They aren't willing to exert the additional time and effort, and in some cases inherit additional risk, to increase their cash flow through these strategies.

Common R2R Strategies

Whilst various R2R strategies exist, I have only regularly come across two main strategies worth covering in this section. These include:

- Rent to Rent HMO, known as R2RHMO or R2HMO
- Rent to Rent Serviced Accommodation, known as R2RSA or R2SA

When someone refers to "R2R", nine times out of ten they are referring to Rent to Rent HMO or simply rent-to-rent in general, as I have above. HMO refers to a *house in multiple occupation*, where multiple tenants will let a bedroom each and share facilities such as a bathroom, kitchen, and garden. Landlords who are looking to enhance their income will often convert their properties into an HMO and let to tenants directly. However, not all landlords are willing to go through this hassle or they have gone through this hassle, but simply have no will to continue. This brings us to R2RHMO. The R2RHMO strategy is the process of renting an entire property from a landlord for a fixed rent, usually 4-bedrooms or more, then letting each room out to a tenant(s) for a period of time under an Assured Short Hold Tenancy (the typical rental tenancy agreement). There is little difference between a landlord and a R2R operator running an HMO to the end tenant; the only difference is that a landlord owns the property, where as a R2R operator rents the property off the landlord. For a R2RHMO operator, the total gross earnings are calculated by summing up the rents of each room (R2 from equation above), which to be successful should exceed the total fixed rent agreed with the landlord (R1 from equation above) minus any operating fees (C1 from equation above). For example, and this is a very simplistic example for the purposes of this introduction, let's assume you agree to rent an entire six-bedroom property from a landlord for

£2000 per month. Assuming the property has an HMO licence, let's say you can let each room out to an individual for £550pcm. Should you let six rooms out, the property will generate £3300pcm, creating a £1300pcm gross profit. If we assume it costs you, the R2R operator, £850pcm to run the property (management fees, repairs, bills etc), then the NET profit of that property shall be £450pcm, excluding tax. Please don't take those numbers as gospel, but for example purposes you can see how profits are generated using this method. From my experience speaking with R2RHMO operators, this approach is fraught with unforeseen costs, repairs, and management issues, causing it to be a time-consuming strategy. This very reason is exactly why profit can be made, as the typical landlord is not willing to exert the additional effort required to generate this additional income. The property needs to be to HMO specification and must be licenced in accordance with local council requirements. R2RHMO is outside of my expertise, so I will leave the summary for this strategy here, but it's another avenue to explore if the serviced accommodation strategy doesn't suit you.

R2RSA is the strategy of renting an entire property through a company for a fixed rent, 1-bedroom or more, and then letting the property out on a short-term basis as a serviced accommodation unit. The term serviced accommodation can be defined as the following:

"Serviced accommodation refers to fully furnished properties that are available to let for primarily short-term durations (up to 90 days). This type of accommodation will typically offer facilities similar to those offered by hotels, as well as kitchen and cleaning services".

The property is essentially marketed as a hotel room, however, the guest benefits from additional services such as a separate living room, a full kitchen, and linen washing facilities. The property is advertised on platforms such as AirBnB & Booking.com, where guests will book to stay in the property, paying the R2RSA operator a nightly rate per night. For a R2RSA property to be successful, the sum of the nightly rates charged, multiplied by the occupancy rate (R2 from equation above), minus the running costs (C1 from equation above) shall exceed the fixed rent agreed with the landlord (R1 from equation above) creating a monthly profit. The net result is that a property will create cash flow through users booking to stay in the property. We will look at financial examples later in this book. <u>Not all properties will yield a profitable investment using R2RSA!</u> There are various factors which will influence a property's success using this strategy which we'll explore throughout this book. But first, let's look at what you will need if you wish to start a R2RSA business. I want to state that the content of this book is solely applicable to the United Kingdom rental market. Although I see nothing blocking the application of this strategy within other countries, I personally have no experience with this and cannot advise whether any local laws will be breached in the process.

Chapter 2 - Begin your R2RSA Journey

If you are reading this book, you are already ahead of most others entering the R2RSA space. I've worked with individuals who entered this strategy with literally no property training or experience. On the contrary, I've worked with very experienced property investors looking to add additional cash flow to their existing property portfolio. In my opinion, before jumping in headfirst, anyone entering the space needs to understand the principles first, which I'll explain to you in this book. However, this book is non-exhaustive, meaning that it doesn't cover every aspect in sufficient depth to start operating immediately. It does, however, give you an excellent platform to develop your understanding and make informed decisions moving forward, of which I hope is valuable to you. Let's look at your options moving forward to gain further knowledge.

Finding the Knowledge

Courses & Mentorship

Courses are currently the leading method of gaining R2RSA knowledge. This is the route I went down, where I was fortunate that I landed with a training provider that did exactly what it said it would do – teach me how to set up and operate an R2RSA business.

I can't speak directly for the quality of other courses, but I can advise that by speaking to other course directors and participants, not all courses on this subject are made equal, nor are they priced equal. The reality is, if you want to expand your knowledge on the subject with experts, you will have to pay for a course, but I would strongly advise that you define your strategy and understand your restrictions using this book before signing up for a course. From my experience, courses range from £1000 - £5000, all coming with different levels of knowledge, durations, and support. I'm happy to provide references to good quality course content, but the goal here is to give you overarching knowledge on the strategy before paying large education fees. This section sub-chapter is prompted by my own experience. I work full-time as an engineer on very demanding, time-critical projects nationwide. Towards the beginning of my R2RSA journey, I was also in my final year of a part-time engineering degree. I did not have material such as this book to advise that it would be a good idea to build a strategy and assess my current constraints prior to jumping into paid mentorship. If I had taken some initial steps, like you are about to, I could have maximised my time with paid mentors and would've known what to expect, which ultimately would have led to greater efficiency, motivation and income. Therefore, I believe you have absolutely done the right thing by reading this book first, and we'll look at the strategies applicable in the following chapters. Whether it's a course I recommend or not, you will most likely come across claims that you will generate £5000 – £10,000 per month within the course duration. I would recommend taking this with a pinch of salt. Don't set your aspirations that high, yet. I found that by having that expectation, it often led to de-motivation, even when I did start generating income. There will be scenarios where an individual on a course may have hit £7500 in sourcing fees on month 2 by finding a rare block of 3 apartments. However, they won't tell you about months 1, 3 and 4 earning considerably less. However, this strategy absolutely has the potential to generate 10K per month with time, dedication, and scaling efficiencies by combining the different income methods of R2RSA, which we'll explore later. People do need courses to learn and some do produce incredibly valuable content. I just believe that in most cases the claims to earn large sums of money in a very short time frame are unrealistic and unsustainable for 99% of the public, but are absolutely achievable over a slightly longer time frame with perseverance and experience.

If you want to find a reliable course, the best way to do this is through word of mouth. There are plenty of R2R Facebook groups with thousands of members of all abilities and experience levels. If you would like to find a course outside of my recommendations, I would suggest posting that you are looking for R2RSA mentorship in these groups. You will no doubt get bombarded by the businesses that offer paid mentorship, which of course you can contact, but initially I would recommend identifying those already on a training course of some kind and asking for their opinion. If you can't find someone specifically on the course, you can always ask the course director to put you in touch with one of their students. Just bear in mind this will most likely be their best-performing student, hence I'm suggesting you try to find a course member outside of the course directors' recommendation. Arrange a call, or even a face-to-face meeting with them to discuss how they found the course content. Understand if the content will suit you, your strategy, and your limitations, of which you'll have clarity on upon completing this book.

Alternatively, some of the training providers have free pages where they will offer condensed content about their R2RSA programme. You will most likely find posts which tag student members who have had a good financial week, so you can message them directly from here.

On the Job Training

If you want to avoid paying for mentorship and company/compliance set-up fees, your alternative option is to start your R2RSA journey by joining an established R2RSA business by offering your time and services. It's common practice for businesses to increase their capacity by bringing in external support. Some businesses will offer full-time positions with salaries, although they will almost certainly be looking for experienced applicants with a sound track record. This won't be suitable for a beginner; however, some businesses will take on inexperienced staff with the intention of training them if they agree to a fully commission-based position. For the business, this is a risk free method of gaining additional support. This way you receive an opportunity to learn core aspects of R2RSA and earn money whilst you do it (instead of spending it on a course), all without any of the initial outlay or risks. A no-brainer, right? Well, there are a few things to bear in mind. As with any employee, it's unlikely you will learn all the aspects of how to run a R2RSA business yourself, it's far more likely you'll be set doing a very specific task for the business. For example, you may just be making calls to letting agents in a specific location, or you may just be sending messages to investors in Facebook groups or through email campaigns. My point is, you will not get the rounded knowledge that a competent course director will offer you, and it'll probably take longer to acquire that knowledge through work experience alone. Also, be prepared to earn absolutely nothing, jack all, zero, for the first few months through your learning stage. Part-time, this isn't so bad but full-time, this can be fairly soul-destroying. However, it's a step you can take to get exposure to the industry with little risk. One side note, even if you set up your own business and receive training, you are still likely to earn very little in the opening couple of months. This is normal, so it's not a hardship which should discourage you. If you again utilise the Facebook groups and search "Hiring", you will most likely come across posts from companies (even myself) who have been looking for staff to come aboard for a specific business purpose. Message these individuals directly and see if they still need support. You won't have much luck finding opportunities on legitimate job application websites, simply because there are very few isolated R2RSA businesses, however, you may well find opportunities within larger property businesses looking for staff who, for example, will search for all property-related investments such as land, below market value buildings, HMO's, apartment blocks etc. Remember, R2RSA is a very niche property strategy, but there are many others which you can investigate outside of this book.

The Essentials

Let's look over the essentials you'll need to start your own R2RSA business. Unfortunately, there is no practical way of getting around these essentials where each of them comes with time and monetary restrictions. However, this is part of the game, so don't be too deterred by these actions – all R2RSA operators have to go through them. Whilst clearly a brief overview, I shall provide far more detail during the remainder of the book content.

You'll need a business.

As a starter for ten, you will need a limited company incorporated through the UK government website. Your company shall be used for taking fees, paying taxes, signing company let agreements, offering management services and far more beyond. If you have never set up a company before, it does seem an intimidating first action, but let me assure you that the process is extremely simple. It's a cheap, step by step process that ultimately leads to your new company being listed on the company house website, with a certificate to prove it. Without a company, you have no chance of landlords or developers working with you or accepting your services as you'll simply look unprofessional, unreliable and you'll be unable to sign company let contracts, the core contract used to acquire R2RSA properties.

You'll need a bank account.

Along with your business, you'll need a company bank account. This will be ground zero for all of your incoming and outgoing funds. Again, the process of setting up a commercial bank account is fairly simple, depending on the financial institution you decide to bank with. Your business will then have the applicable banking details to receive and send payments, critical for the operation of your business.

You'll need some form of existing reliable income and act as a personal guarantor for the business.

As you are a new company with no reputation or company accounts, any R2RSA properties you acquire through letting agents or landlords will more than likely require a personal guarantor through what's called the referencing process. This is a financial check on the personal guarantor to see if they can afford the rental figure in the event the company becomes bankrupt or liquidated. In most cases, this will be yourself if you're in employment, a business partner or even a family member who meets the referencing criteria. A typical referencing check will review the income of a personal guarantor, where a pass will be achieved if the guarantor's yearly salary exceeds 30 times the rent. For example, if you rent a property for £1000 PCM, then you'll typically need to earn a £30,000/year gross salary to pass the affordability check. If you plan on sourcing or managing R2RSA properties for other clients/businesses, then the client's business will need to provide a personal guarantor. You only need a personal guarantor if your company is signing for properties via company let agreements. The guarantor is often requested as start-up companies in the past have agreed to a 36-month contract, fallen behind on rental payments, then dissolved the company to write off any debt. This process has caused significant financial loss to landlords, therefore the requirement for a personal guarantor has become far more common. In the very rare case, you may come across a particular landlord who, for whatever reason, doesn't perform referencing checks. Whilst this is possible, I wouldn't hold your breath, as these landlords are few and far between and the quantity is reducing as time goes on.

Your business needs to be compliant.

Compliance is fundamental for any R2RSA business. Not only does it ensure you're abiding by the law, but it also shows other businesses, landlords or developers that you are operating professionally with the correct protection. Compliance comes in different forms, and the level of protection measures (i.e. value of insurance, type of insurance etc.) put in place for a business can vary depending on the directors preferences.

You'll need some capital.

Almost all businesses need some start-up capital, your R2RSA business is no different. You will initially need to fund your compliance costs, which will vary depending on the strategy you are implementing. Subsequently, you will need to fund property acquisitions (sourcing fees, furniture, management setup fees etc.) management systems, a website and potentially further education. The total amount of start-up capital required will also vary depending on your strategy, which we'll review in the next chapter.

You may want a website.

This step is optional; however, I'm including it in the essentials because I've always found it good practice to refer landlords and letting agents to my website for further information about my business and frequently asked questions. Furthermore, you come across as increasingly professional and legitimate with a presentable website, demonstrating your compliance details along with your services. I've also had leads originate from people finding my website with very little marketing, so I see it as a no-brainer.

You can get a website made online by a professional developer for as little as £50-£100 using websites such as Fiverr. I made my own using Wix, which you can see at the Studley Properties website.

You'll need determination – and lots of it!

This really is the most important step of all. It's free but critical to making R2RSA succeed. Remember those less honest people I referred to in Chapter 1? Well, they continue to thrive in this strategy, and the more they do, the fewer people will be willing to work with those trusted operators, and the harder it becomes to find investments where landlords and letting agents are on board.

I've got an exercise for you. Call one or two estate agents and position yourself as a house purchaser, looking to purchase an additional property, expanding your investment portfolio with them. Carefully note how you are treated – 9 times out of 10 it'll be a very pleasant experience.

Now, a couple of days later, call again but this time as a business owner looking to rent some of their properties using a company let agreement for serviced accommodation. 9 times out of 10 it'll be much less pleasant, and they'll quickly show you the metaphorical door. You are literally on their doorstep offering them business and they are rejecting it. Why? –Because the letting agents have heard this pitch before, and it hasn't gone well for them. From the agent's point of view, you're just another R2RSA pitch acting as a one-way ticket to them losing a trusted landlord's business. It's a shame, but it's reality.

My point is, you're going to come across a lot of rejection throughout your journey, so determination is critical to persevere through the noise. However, please don't start a R2RSA business, put in the dedication, perseverance and start then operating with dishonesty and lack of remorse. This is really not something the industry needs right now in its fragile state.

Don't believe me about the state of R2RSA right now? – maybe I'm triggering a few R2RSA operators and sourcers by saying this, but this problem is real and being reported on major platforms. For example, head over to my favourite podcast, The Property Hub Podcast which is one of the largest property-based podcasts nationwide. You would think they would be on board with their fellow property investors in the R2R sector. Nope. Listen to episode TTP475 from 1:25 – 5:32. I had to listen to this on my early morning journey to the office and it saddened me, but as I'm sure you have gathered by now, I completely agree with their comments.

Chapter 3 – Defining your Strategy

Now that you have a very basic understanding of the essentials, we can look at tailoring a strategy for you based on your personal commitments and time restrictions. We'll first look at the methods used by R2RSA operators to generate income through their businesses.

Income Generation Methods

There are three core ways of generating income through this strategy. Each requires different skill sets, time requirements and inherited risk levels. Most R2RSA companies will utilise a combination of these methods to diversify their income, which we'll explore when we look at tailored strategies later on.

Method 1 - Operating your own R2RSA Properties

Method 2 - Managing R2RSA properties

Method 3 - Sourcing R2RSA properties for investors

As I introduce the income strategies, I'm keeping the descriptions as concise and as simple as possible for introductory purposes, but rest assured we'll dive into the strategies in more depth in subsequent chapters.

Method 1 - Operating your own R2RSA properties

The first income generating method is having R2RSA properties in your company's portfolio. As described within Chapter 1, your company will rent a property from a landlord using a Company Let contact, furnish and stage the property for serviced accommodation use, list the property online via Airbnb or Booking.com, then receive bookings from guests on a nightly rate basis. If any of the terms I have used above are unclear at the moment, do not worry as I will be covering these in more detail throughout this book. Using Method 1, you can expect to earn positive monthly cash flow from each of your R2RSA properties as guests book to stay through online travel agencies. Assuming your property is well positioned geographically, demands strong nightly rates and yields high occupancy, which we'll deep dive into throughout the coming chapters, it should continue to provide positive cash flow year-round for the duration of your contract, with the odd negative month expected in those less desirable periods (often January). There is no limit to the quantity of R2RSA properties of which you can hold in your company's portfolio. You should define a limit based on your cash reserves and risk tolerance. The monthly financial return produced by each property will not be a constant figure each month, fluctuating based on guest demand in the area, price re-adjustments and varying running costs. The set-up and ongoing management of your properties can be done yourself if you wish to maximise profitability. Alternatively, management can be outsourced although you should expect lower monthly profits and higher initial investment, ultimately reducing your ROI. This is another example of the time-profit trade-off outlined in Chapter 1.

Method 2 – Managing R2RSA properties

The ability to manage R2RSA properties is a great asset to your business. Not only do you have the ability to manage your investments, but you also can charge a management fee when managing properties for alternative companies. At the time of writing, a typical management company will charge in the region of 15 – 20% of the gross income generated by a property (minus bills) plus VAT where applicable. If you're managing your properties, you will achieve a higher return on investment by minimising your expenses. By managing a client's property, you can charge in the region of a 15 – 20% fee, risk-free. When I say risk-free, I mean that as a management company you're not liable for paying any rent or bills, you could operate a sole management company and have next to zero expenditures within your business. You could also use management income to offset some of the risk of property acquisition through rent liability. Management fees are often calculated on the gross income of a R2RSA property, often leading to quite substantial fees earned through management services. Management is absolutely a tool of which can be used to build a high cash flowing business.

I may have given the impression from my last paragraph that management is an easy, quick way to build a high cash flow business. But before we get too excited, there are a few points to remember with R2RSA management. Poor management looks like this:

- Creating listings on AirBnB and Booking.com
- Wait for bookings
- Go to the pub

This is not how to effectively manage. Managing in this reactive style will not maximise your portfolio's returns and will lead to a lack of bookings in the long term. In the later chapters I will advocate proactive management, which looks like this:

- Optimise the properties quality through professional photos and soft furnishings
- Creating a listing on AirBnB and Boooking.com through a channel management software
- Contact local businesses and offer accommodation for their staff
- Partner with local businesses offering incentives for their customers, local restaurants etc
- Actively check in and respond to guests, offering them local guidance for fun activities and quality restaurants

- Optimising client returns and providing cash flow reports to them monthly
- Replenishing properties and ensuring cleaning is performed to the correct standard
- Managing a team of cleaners, handymen and virtual assistants ensuring business functionality
- Performing property setups and damage spot checks
- Finding, meeting and discussing opportunities with new clients to build your portfolio

Suddenly we can see that good management becomes reasonably labour-intensive. And that's why a management company can demand a generous fee. You guessed it; earning risk-free management fees comes at a trade-off with time. Subsequently, managing a series of properties becomes a full-time occupation, especially during the initial stage of your management journey. We'll dive deeper into how to manage properties effectively in the following chapters.

Method 3 - Sourcing R2RSA properties for investors

Sourcing R2RSA properties is the process of physically searching the rental market looking for properties which are suitable for the R2RSA strategy. A sourcer will earn a sourcing fee for the time and effort they have put into finding and securing the property, performing all the necessary financial and statutory checks, and passing the investment on to a keen investor, who is looking to build their portfolio using Method 1 described earlier. Subsequently, the sourcer has no further input or connection to that property. At the time of writing, a single standalone R2RSA investment sourcing fee may range from £1500 to £3000 per property. If an individual is charging over this, they best be able to provide strong evidence proving to you that the property will provide a stronger ROI than normal. If an individual is charging less than this, there is normally a reason for it, which is up to you to determine. A sourcing company able to source properties consistently for investors will be generating healthy cash flow with little risk as, similar to a management company, the sourcer is not liable for any fee or rental payments.

We'll discuss sourcing in more depth in subsequent chapters but trust me when I say sourcing is not a case of finding a property on Rightmove, making a call, securing the property and banking £3000. It's incredibly labour-intensive and will have you at your knees some days. In my opinion, since sourcers essentially find the property, earn a large fee and have no ongoing interest in its performance (as they gain no additional profit based on its success), you can quite easily come across dis-genuine sourcers. To line their own pockets, these sourcers will try to sell any investment to anyone, usually beginners that don't know any better. I'm not going to accuse these types of sourcers of selling investments they know will not perform financially, but I do believe that they don't check the financial projection thoroughly which can lead to financially poor investments. I'll stress again that these individuals are putting a bad name against those trustworthy sourcers operating in the space. I have also come across scenarios where sourcers make "fake investments" advertising them to investors. Then, they have found a keen investor who is happy to pay a sourcing fee, secured it from them, then the sourcer has disappeared. Sourcing fee scams are a real problem in the industry so do some thorough research into the sourcing company's legitimacy prior to sending sourcing fees. I believe that sourcing is the most time-intensive income generation method of the three options presented above, but it can be a great way of making larger sums of capital for your business in a relatively short period of time.

Core Restrictions

Now that you have a basic understanding of the different ways to generate income within your business, let's look at the key restrictions which will define which income-generation methods will best suit you.

Time

Remember the time/effort correlation chart in Chapter 1? This guides the R2RSA sector. Your time is a commodity which is traded for cash flow in all of the strategies defined in this section. Simply put, the more time you can assign to R2RSA, the more money you'll make, on average, over the medium to long term. I have neglected the short term here because, even if you work at this for a couple of months full time, you may simply get unlucky either failing to find an opportunity or having opportunities fall through via actions outside of your control. Have you ever heard the phrase – *the harder you work, the luckier you get*? I believe this to be true, which is why I say over the medium to long term, you'll perform well if you continue to put the effort in.

You need to be honest with yourself about how much time you can assign to the strategy. Let me give you an example from my experience. When I'm interviewing a potential sourcer to work within my business and they already have some form of employment, I ask them how much time they are willing to commit to sourcing. Amongst the excitement, I have had some individuals commit their entire weekends and evenings to sourcing as they are keen to earn large commissions. Can't blame them, right? When I've gone down this road in the past, individuals working within my business have devoted most of their free time to sourcing, made no leads, and within as little as a week, quit. This is because they completely underestimate the difficulty but also committed too much of their spare time, making it unsustainable.

Make a realistic commitment. If you work full time like me, you can get up early and do a couple of hours in the morning as I do. Maybe 4 hours on a Saturday morning? Sure – but I wouldn't personally suggest budgeting an additional 30 hours around your full-time occupation to pursue a R2RSA business. But you do you – If you truly want to do that, and it works out well for you, then I'll hold my hands up. I'm only speaking from experience. The other thing to consider is at what time during the day you assign time to your R2RSA business. This is important as if you're looking to source your properties, you are at an advantage if you can align this time with when letting agents are open. You can work out of hours messaging agents through email, but I've found the hit rate on a message to an agent is very limited, especially as most of them are defensive when it comes to R2RSA inquiries. Even when you do message/email agents, assuming they don't ignore you, you'll be littered with call's during working hours asking for more information, so you'll be disrupted from your other commitments either way. Note down how many hours you can assign, what days those hours are on and when those hours are going to be. For me, as an example, the time restrictions of only having a couple of hours on a morning and evening have told me that sourcing and managing seriously are going to be difficult as they are time intensive strategies.

Capital

Depending on what income generation techniques you are operating within your business, varying amounts of start-up capital will be required. This guide is only a guide, not a hard and fast rule. I believe it to be accurate as of the time of writing. I'm speaking from experience; however, prices change. You may require less capital, you may require more. This section is purely to demonstrate the general costs for a typical start-up R2RSA company.

Compliance

Compliance is the first expenditure a R2RSA company will inherit. We talk more about what compliance is and why it's important later on, but here we'll simply look at the estimated capital requirements.

Compliance Requirement	Cost
Property Redress Scheme Membership (other options are available)	£135-£220
Information Commission Office	£40
Anti-Money Laundering	£300
Company Liability Insurance (Quote Required)	£80-£140
Company Indemnity Insurance (Quote Required)	£200-£300
Estimated Total	**£1000**
Estimated Total + VAT	**£1200**

Table 1 – Estimated Compliance Costs

The reason I'm demonstrating a range for some costs is that there are a few decisions you will need to make about what level of protection you are wanting to operate under. For example, you may choose to take out a higher degree of insurance than I have, therefore, your insurance costs will exceed mine. There are personal decisions that you as a business director will need to make, which I don't plan on influencing. Another limitation of Table 1 is that some of the costs already include VAT, while others don't. To keep things simple, I've applied VAT to the total figure, so there is a good chance £1200 will be a slight overestimate. When I last applied for my compliance documentation, the total summed to £900.66, however institutions have recently indicated an increase in membership prices, so by the time you come around to applying for your compliance, the estimate in Table 1 shall provide you with a reliable estimate. Note that these figures are annual subscriptions, so you will have rolling costs yearly to maintain your company's compliance.

Method 1 – Capital Requirement

When setting up your own R2RSA properties within your company, you will inherit the setting up costs needed to take that property from its current state to being listed on the Online Travel Agencies (AirBnB etc). I will start this section by saying that not all properties are equal, so no one rule fits all of which you can apply to each property. Your ability to deploy more of your own time into your property acquisition and set-up will lessen your set-up costs.

I'm going to use a typical 2-bedroom apartment in Manchester as the baseline example for this section, an incredibly popular R2RSA investment area at the time of writing. We'll assume that the agreed rent for this property is £1300 for example purposes. Costs will fluctuate depending on the location, size and condition of a property. The only way to get an accurate cost for any property that you find is to physically cost it, which I'll take you through in subsequent chapters, but at least this section will inform you of the high-level costs to expect during acquisition. The below table demonstrates some of the costs you may incur when setting up a R2RSA property.

Typical 2-Bedroom Apartment Set-up	Cost
Sourcing Fee	£1500-3000
Furniture Fee	£3000 - 5000
First Month's Rent *(July 2022 Rates)*	£1300
Deposit *(usually 4-weeks rent)*	£1300
Management set-up fee	£300 - 600
Property Insurance	£100 - 150
Noise Detector	£100
Lock Box	£30-50
Estimated Total	**£11,500**

Table 2 – Estimated Set Up Costs

The above cost is completely flexible. If you source the property yourself then you can eliminate the sourcing fee. If your property is already furnished by the landlord to a high specification, then you can reduce your furniture expenditure by installing only soft furnishings to improve the property's aesthetics, costing a fraction of a full furniture fit-out. You may be able to negotiate a zero-deposit contract, or at the very worst, get your deposit back at the end of your term if the property is still in satisfactory condition. You can set up your unit yourself to eliminate your management set-up fee. On the other hand, the landlord may want an 8-week deposit as they see the flow of regular guests entering their property as an additional risk, or they may increase the rental figure for company tenant's full stop. I'm also increasingly seeing some letting agents wanting a piece of the pie, asking for upfront fees specifically charged for a company let application. The point is, I can't give you accurate costs without seeing the property and doing a full assessment - each property needs to be assessed individually.

Some good news though, I'll demonstrate how this can be done in later chapters. What I will say with certainty is that you will be doing very well to set up any R2RSA unit for less than £4000 - £5000. I'd consider that a minimum capital requirement, but it may well take months to find that elusive low capital investment in the rough.

Method 2 & 3 – Capital Requirement

Aside from compliance costs described earlier, methods 2 & 3 essentially have no upfront capital requirements. As your business grows, you'll most likely start to use various software packages which allow your company to manage more clients more efficiently. These will come at a cost in the form of a monthly subscription, however, are quite negligible. I would recommend investing in knowledge through training or mentorship allowing you to perform these activities, but it's only your time that you will need to invest to start generating income using these methods. Method 2, sourcing, can be done effectively without any paid tools at all, making the upfront capital requirement even lower, but as described earlier, this comes with a higher time commitment.

Strategy Recommendations

The reality is that most R2RSA companies will combine each of the income generation methods described creating a diversified income stream. Now that you have identified your time and capital restrictions, we can explore what strategy will be best for you. What I can't do in this section is go through every single combination of time and capital restriction conceivable and give recommendations on each one. That will simply take far too long. Here are some more generalised recommendations which will hopefully inspire you to consider the most feasible direction for your business.

Scenario One – Limited Time & Capital

If you have come to R2RSA with very little time (<2 hours/day) or capital to invest (<£4000), then, unfortunately, it's my opinion that you aren't yet ready to enter this space. The time/profit trade-off demonstrated in Figure 1 is exactly that, a trade-off. Without anything to trade, you simply don't have sufficient leverage to start earning an income through R2RSA. I'm not suggesting that it's impossible to generate any income through R2RSA with your current limitations, but without capital, you can't utilise Method 1, and Methods 2 & 3 are time-sensitive strategies, where you're essentially creating yourself an additional job. You may get lucky and find a property with your very limited time which passes all financial and statutory checks. You could then proceed to try to sell this to an investor, but there are further obstacles after finding the property which will trip you up if you don't have sufficient time flexibility to attend to them immediately.

I'm not a qualified lifestyle advisor, but I'll echo those who are much more qualified than I am. If you want to get more involved with R2RSA, or investment in general, do what you can to rationale expenses, leaving yourself in a positive cash flow position after each pay-check, and accumulate funds to get yourself in a position where you can start to use your capital as a trade-off to acquire cash flowing assets such as those described in Method 1. On a side note, it's probably debatable whether a rented property can be defined as an "asset". Since it takes money from your business, it may be defined better as a positive cash-flowing liability. If you find yourself struggling to build additional capital, then you will be forced to assign more time to R2RSA if you want to improve your chances of success. Unfortunately, without knowing your personal circumstances, I can't advise on how you can achieve this. It simply comes down to prioritisation, understanding which time you're willing to sacrifice to assign to further income generation.

Your primary challenge is going to be saving your capital as well as finding additional time to explore some of the following scenarios.

Scenario Two – Limited Time with Disposable Capital

Scenario two best describes my position, where I have disposable capital assigned to R2RSA (>£4000) but I don't have sufficient time to go into the depth necessary to consistently source and manage properties. If you too are in a similar position, then I would recommend using Method 1 as the primary source of income generation by acquiring R2RSA investments. By using Method 1, you are letting your properties do the work for you, generating income with little interface from yourself.

When I say "limited time" this is different for each person. If like me, you want nothing to do with your property and just want to see returns, I would recommend finding a good quality management company that will deal with the day-to-day guest management etc. I have a property now that I have never been to, never intend to go to, and have never spoken with, dealt with or even acknowledged a guest who has stayed. It is as hands-off as hands-off can get. This is only possible because I have a reliable management company in place that I wholeheartedly trust, and they do a great job. I pay them out of the property's profits for this luxury. You could also explore trying to manage your units yourself, but to be honest, I find that a good management company can increase your property's income to a point where you will generate the same income whilst paying them a management fee. This is assuming that because you have limited time you can't manage proactively, responding to guests and advertising the property at the same level a quality management company can.

With your limited time, in my opinion, Methods 2 & 3 still are not practical for sustained income. Don't get me wrong, with my limited time I have successfully used Method 3 to source units for investors, earning healthy sourcing fees in the process. But the time I assigned outside of working hours to make this happen, along with the constant disruption throughout my day job from emails and WhatsApp messages from my investors, letting agents and members of my team were simply not worth it for me. However, it might be for you, but these are just my thoughts.

With regards to Method 2, again, with your limited time you can't be responsive to guests' needs nor can you be very proactive throughout the working day, so I wouldn't recommend trying to set up a management company in this scenario at least at the beginning of your R2RSA journey.

Your primary challenge will be finding deal sourcers and a management company that you trust, avoiding sourcing fee scammers at all costs. If you're struggling, you can email me and I can recommend some companies that you can start some initial conversations with.

Scenario Three – Time Rich with Limited Capital

Scenario Three may be more applicable for the younger generation reading this book, where you find yourself with limited capital, but ample time to look into utilising those strategies with low initial capital investment. Let's say you are studying at university, or you work part-time, then you have a great opportunity to learn and trade your time for income. Once you have built some capital, you can then look at reducing your time input by pursuing the less time-intensive strategies.

If you're new to R2RSA, then I would recommend that you start with Method 3. The rationale for this is that you will naturally meet investors, other sourcers and management companies through the regular day-to-day communication involved with sourcing, and it will broaden your contact list as well as your experience in the sector. This will put you in a better position to start a management company using Method 2 further down the line. You might be thinking at this point – *"Didn't this guy have a rant earlier in this book about inexperienced people sourcing and now he's recommending that's exactly what I do"?* Well, yes, but you are going to be different as you are going to understand the truth about sourcing R2RSA units from the start of your journey after this book. I, therefore, have confidence that you will be sourcing in the morally correct way, which I have no issues with. Your strategy could be to go hell for leather into sourcing, putting as much feasible time into it as possible, looking for those investments that investors will bite your hand off for.

When you decide to explore Method 2, you now will have some basic contacts and investors who, like myself, may well be looking for fully managed investments. You can offer an in-house management service along with your sourced investments, which is often attractive to investors as it shortens the communication chain between the investment, the sourcer and the management company. To start with, you will get away with managing one or two units without the support of many systems in place, however, as your business builds you will need to look into streamlining your management services which we'll look into in later chapters. Using Method Three, you will be very busy, constantly trawling through online letting services and dealing with investor communication. However, since you're putting the time in, you will see the most extensive income generation of the scenarios so far if performed successfully.

Your primary challenges will be finding properties which pass statutory and financial checks, whilst finding investors who trust you to source and manage their properties with your little experience. You may well have to charge an introductory management fee, or reduced sourcing fee, considerably below market rate as an incentive to get your first client through the door.

Quick tip – if you find an investment that has high investor demand, such as a two-bedroom apartment in central Manchester as used in the example earlier, don't be afraid to charge a full market rate sourcing fee even if it's your first property. If the investor market is hot, it'll most likely sell.

Scenario Four – Time Rich with Disposable Capital

If you're in this scenario and keen to invest using the R2RSA methods, then you're in a great position to get started. You have the option of picking and choosing your methods based on preference as you have no restrictions. I would recommend trying all three methods one way or another, maximising your income through diversification. You can use your funds to start building a cash flow machine through your own properties, and your time to source properties for investors and earn management fees from those less hands-on individuals. One major benefit you have is the time to manage your properties, saving the management fee and maximising your profit each month. You will face the same challenges as those in the other scenarios, but you have the benefit of having additional time and funds to support your success. It's worth noting though, just because you have the funds and time to successfully build a R2RSA business, doesn't mean you should. Maybe you are looking to deploy capital into R2RSA as an additional means of income, but want to focus your time on other non-R2R investments. In this case, you could look to explore Scenario 2 exclusively. The point is, you have plenty of options.

Aside from the challenges already listed in the other scenarios, your challenge will be not getting caught up in the excitement and deploying your funds and time wisely in the areas of the strategies which pique your interest. Do your best to avoid those less genuine sourcers and managers along your journey as they will happily pocket your hard-earned funds themselves.

Chapter 4 – Understanding the Risks

If you read any investment or financial-oriented literature, you will commonly come across statements along the lines of *"please be aware of the risks before investing"* or *"We are not liable for any financial loss due to the contents of this…"*. This is because all investments carry a level of risk, but not all investments are born equal. In my opinion, I would say that R2R, specifically Serviced Accommodation (SA), carries the highest level of risk of any property-related investment strategy available to common retail investors like myself. It must be said, however, high risk – high reward is certainly a factual statement in the current market which brings high profits. There are certain methods used to mitigate these risks, so it's vitally important to understand both the risks and mitigation to make financially educated decisions in this space. In this section I'll explain why I believe this strategy is particularly risky, highlighting the most prominent risks associated with this strategy and how I mitigate them, allowing you to conclude whether your personal risk tolerance allows you to utilise this strategy.

The Risk of Negative Cash Flow

When operating your R2RSA properties in your company name, there are going to be some risks implied to either yourself or the personal guarantor you have selected. Let me make something clear – if you are renting a property under your businesses name and you are the personal guarantor, then you are liable to pay that rent every month without fail unless one of three actions are performed:

- Your contract/term length finishes
- Either you or the landlord actions a break clause

- The contract is terminated through non-compliance to the contract's terms and conditions

Note that each contract is different, and it's your responsibility to check the terms before signing, but the above is a list of common methods used to terminate contracts.

In a worst-case scenario, if you don't get sufficient bookings/income to cover the rent and ongoing pre-agreed costs, you may well be in negative equity each month and the investment will deplete your wealth, not build it. Unlike traditional property strategies or even the R2RHMO strategy, a large section of the market is individuals who book to stay in serviced accommodation for non-essential reasons. Therefore, if there was an economic downturn for example, or let's say a pandemic, bookings may well reduce significantly putting you into negative equity. On the contrary, the B2L or R2RHMO strategy caters for living space; people always need somewhere to live no matter the economic state. This fact alone I feel makes R2RSA far less bulletproof. Clearly, this is a major risk. You cannot just walk away like selling a stock when it's down, you, or your personal guarantor, will by law be required to pay your monthly liabilities. Failure to do this may lead to legal action unless you have an extremely forgiving landlord. It's worth noting however that this risk is applicable to other property strategies as well. I've re-visited this section as the second and third quarters of 2022 have experienced interest rate hikes, thus lending/mortgage rate hikes, in the But-to-Let market. Landlords looking to re-finance, who haven't stress tested their properties during acquisition, are also finding themselves in negative equity scenarios. Despite this risk sounding dramatic, it's certainly not unique to R2RSA, it's only the rationale for the negative equity which changes between the strategies.

Negative Cashflow Mitigation

I have highlighted an extreme case, but it could be your reality if you aren't careful. So, how do we mitigate this? The key mitigation is to maximise the likelihood of getting regular bookings each month, all year round. Selecting a high-demand area to set up your R2RSA properties is the best method of achieving this. You want to select an area that will experience bookings from various clients for a selection of reasons, diversifying your chances of getting a booking. For example, by selecting a location like central York, you are tapping into two key markets: contractors and tourism. In this case, you have selected a location which will experience bookings through businesses and corporations all year round. In addition to this, the area is desirable for tourism, where tourists visiting the area for leisure will also be booking your apartment. The net result, you tapped into diversified markets stacking the deck in your favour, reducing your risk. You will be more exposed to risk if, for example, you acquired a lodge in the Yorkshire dales. Now, you are entirely reliant on guests booking your lodge for leisure purposes only as, lets be honest, very little business occurs in the dales. This completely removes the contractor market from your prospective guests. Contractors are a key target market as even during economic down turns businesses still need employees to travel the country to conduct commercial activities. If you have purely focused on tourism guests, and for whatever reason people don't want to stay in the countryside or are simply reducing their expenditure due to economic reasons, your property could sit vacant for weeks.

Another way to mitigate this risk is by producing a listing which excels on booking platforms such as AirBnB or Booking.com. Setting your property up with your guests in mind, you can include additional services such as Netflix, high-speed internet, high-quality furnishings, sofa beds or additional parking facilities to make your property more desirable. Using professional photos combined with well-written descriptions instantly makes your property more attractive to potential clients. Selecting a great management company which you trust will bring these benefits by default. Speaking of management, as your property becomes established, your reviews will play a considerable role in the algorithms, presenting your property nearer the top of the booking platforms if you have strong reviews, thus, increasing your bookings. This is why I was hammering home the importance of good management; it really will increase the property's performance and enhance reviews resulting in more regular bookings and higher cash flow.

The Risk of Early Termination

The risk of early termination is a very real risk that can unfortunately lead to financial loss for R2RSA operators. As we have already discussed in Chapter 3, capital investment is required during the setup of a property, some of which can be quite small, in the region of £4000 - £8000, but easily exceeding £12,000 for larger properties. Most contracts will have some form of break clause included, allowing either party to cancel the contract at a specific point in time without question. Why would a break clause get activated by a landlord? There are various reasons, but to list a few:

- They are getting noise complaints from neighbours due to parties
- Guests are causing damage to the property
- They are looking to sell the property
- They are no longer comfortable with a company let tenant

Either way, if your contract is terminated early for one reason or another, you may find yourself in a position where you have not made back your initial investment, causing a net loss. Break clauses can be set at various durations, I've seen some as short as three months, and others at two years. Ultimately, if you accept a break clause in your contract for less than your targeted investment repayment time, you run the risk of losing your investment even after months of hard work.

Early Termination Mitigation

Early termination can never be fully mitigated as landlords may well change their minds due to unforeseen circumstances, however, we can reduce the risk implied by the issues we can foresee.

Regular parties and damage to a property are two common ways for serviced accommodation operators to ruin their relationship with landlords. Guests will indeed use serviced accommodation to host parties of which it's clear that very little regard is given to the property's condition. This is unfortunately part of the business, however, there are deterrents you can deploy. You can install a Minut noise detector device within the property as the first mitigation action. These devices do not record conversations or breach privacy rights, but they do monitor pre-determined decibel levels and connect to an application on your smartphone, allowing you to monitor noise levels within the property. If you advertise that these devices are present within the property, it's an effective deterrent. In addition to this, you have the option to charge refundable deposits during the booking process on the online booking platforms. Don't be afraid to do this, in most cases guests do understand and will pay it, whereas those unwilling to pay these deposits may well be the problem causers - it's simply not worth the risk.

If you're looking to maintain a positive relationship with a landlord in general, then I'd recommend being responsive, helpful, understanding, and willing to negotiate. If they have a query or problem, deal with it immediately. If your property is exceeding expected returns, share profits with your landlord. This will put your business in a position where you can operate across more of their portfolio as landlords will likely allow you to pick up more of their properties and/or recommend you to another landlord. If they do get complaints from neighbours, for example, they are far less likely to take serious action if you have built a strong win-win relationship with them. I have sourced a property in the past where the investor was incredibly reasonable and polite during the acquisition stage of the investment. However, the moment they received the keys they became very unpleasant, unwilling to solve guest problems, nor did they go to any effort to resolve noise complaints at the property. The net result, the landlord wanted them out immediately claiming breach of contract. To this day I feel embarrassed about this situation and it's not one I wish to repeat. The point being, if that investor continued to keep up pleasantries and responded in a non-offensive manner, they would've stood a much better chance of not having their contract terminated early.

Chapter 5 – Setting up your Business

Now that we have explored what R2RSA is, you understand the key risks and you have a strategy defined based on your restrictions, it's time to get to the fun part. From here on out, we'll explore how to build a R2RSA business. Finally, I'll explain where I think the future of serviced accommodation is heading nationwide, including how I plan to use the strategy within my overall investment portfolio over the medium term. The goal is to lay out my truth around this strategy, hopefully giving you the information you need to make informed decisions throughout your own R2RSA investment career.

Choosing a Company Name

If you're looking to pursue this strategy, the first thing you will need is a company and thus a company name. If you have never made a company before I can assure you that it's a simple process.

You need to head over to the government website using the link in the end of book resources, where there is, at the time of writing, a 7-step-by-step guide to follow when creating your company.

I have never come across a R2RSA company that isn't a limited company (Ltd or Limited). Incorporating as a limited company gives you the flexibility to distribute shares amongst business partners and assign various directors. Multiple directors within the business can come in handy for passing some of the more thorough company referencing checks used by landlords and letting agents. If for some reason you don't want to file for a limited company, then seek out advice from a qualified solicitor with R2R experience if you want to explore different trading styles (i.e. sole trader).

The most time-consuming part of creating a company is choosing a company name. If you're like me, I guarantee you already have about five in your back pocket and they sound great, but I also guarantee they'll already be taken. A great website I used is called *namecheckr*. This will check your company name against the social media platforms and registered domain names, telling you if your company name has been taken on other platforms aside from the government's website. To finalise my company name, I had namecheckr open on one screen and the government website open on another, running through various names until I found a promising one that was available on all platforms.

The remainder of the steps are personal decisions of which I don't intend to influence. Once you have completed these steps, you shall receive a certificate confirming your registration. You will also have to register with HMRC for Corporation Tax which again you can find guidance for throughout the government website.

Setting up your Business Bank Account

As touched on earlier, you will need a company bank account to send and receive funds. If you're just getting started, I'd recommend using Tide Ltd. Tide is an online bank that offers free business start-up accounts including a certain level of FSCS protection on your funds. I use Tide and have come across very little resistance when setting up my business account within Tide's system. I found that high street banks were looking for a detailed business plan and generally made me jump through more hoops during application. Of course, there are many other banking options so feel free to pick a banking system at your own will.

Becoming Compliant

Compliance is a subject which appears to cause mass confusion within the industry. Even if you ask some of the R2R "experts" within the industry - *"do you need to be compliant for all R2RSA activities and is it law?"* 99% of the time you will receive a woolly response not directly answering the question.

The problem is that R2RSA is not a widely established strategy which, as of the time of writing, is somewhat unregulated. Therefore, very little official guidance can be found aside from that described by the content within property networking websites and the content I have learnt through paid mentorship. With most of the compliance relating schemes focusing primarily on property sales and the regulation of estate agency firms, us R2RSA sourcers and operators are in a grey area of which it's hard to get a concrete response, even from the scheme operators themselves, as to whether we should apply for their services.

Therefore, I'm going to caveat this section by suggesting that the following compliance information is only a recommendation on my part, where I'm very much reporting in a "monkey see, monkey do" format from the material I have been taught. What I can say with absolute confidence is that I know R2RSA operators also perform their activities under the same compliance institutions, so you will be following the crowd if you also apply the compliance guidance I am about to discuss.

Property Ombudsman or Property Redress Scheme

The Property Ombudsman and the Property Redress Scheme (PRS) are customer redress schemes, authorised to be an impartial service provider who can assist with property-related disputes and complaints between two or more parties.

As part of your compliance, you do not need to be a member of both the Property Ombudsman and the PRS; one membership will suffice. Feel free to read through their website's content and make a decision for yourself as to which scheme you prefer. Fortunately, I have never had to use the PRS to resolve an issue so I can't speak first-hand as to how efficiently their services will resolve a conflict, however, here is the PRS's commitment to its members:

"We aim to help everyone understand their position in relation to the problem by sharing our knowledge and working to reach a fair and reasonable outcome for both parties, quickly and efficiently, as an alternative to the option of going to court. We believe in delivering expert customer service and raising standards in our specialist sectors"

Where I see the most value in these services is that customers can contact the schemes and complain if they think they are being treated incorrectly by an agent or scheme member. I think this is great, as those maybe less educated in how the property market works have protection through the scheme, discouraging those less honest individuals from attempting to pull the wool over customers' eyes. It's worth noting however that these redress schemes are not enforcement agencies.

To become a member, simply visit the respective website, choose a plan, and follow the instructions through to payment. It really is as simple as that, where your membership information will be provided to your company's registered office.

On the contrary to this, to quote the government website, the requirement to join the PRS/Property Ombudsman scheme is applicable, at the time of writing, to the following business's:

- *"an estate agent dealing with residential properties in the UK"*
- *"a letting agent or property manager in England or Wales"*

The consequence of not complying, *"You may be fined up to £5,000 and have your licence revoked if you do not join a redress scheme"*.

The description of the above businesses is different to that of a R2RSA business, no matter what strategy you are deploying. Certainly, if you insured your business labelling yourself as an estate agent or property management company, your insurance would not be valid. The consequence of having your licence revoked is also not applicable to R2RSA, as licences are not attained for our business strategy. This further cements my earlier point that it's not clear whether this type of compliance is really required for R2RSA operators, however, as a precaution I do maintain a membership to inform investors and other operators that we take compliance and customer support, through the use of the PRS scheme, seriously.

Company Insurance

Insurance is essential when operating a business as it acts as a critical safety net in the event that the worst case happens. I will define the key insurance types required as part of compliance documentation; however please get advice from a professional insurance broker who will provide far more detailed advice than I possibly can around the types and level of insurance you require for your business and properties. I can recommend the Insurance Desk as I know that they provide specific R2RSA insurance. <u>Do not insure your company through a cheap comparison website and select the closest option to your business's operations, which will most likely be an estate/letting agency</u>. The website will allow you to purchase the insurance, but in the event of a claim, you will not receive the support you expected as you are not a letting agency. To acquire the correct insurance, simply contact insurance-desk and specifically let them know that you are a Rent to Rent Serviced Accommodation business looking for Public Liability and Indemnity insurance. This way you will be provided with the correct insurance policies for your business. I'll briefly explain the rationale for each type of insurance you may require depending on your strategy.

Public Liability Insurance

Public Liability Insurance offers protection against any claims that arise from damage or injury made by any third party such as customers or clients. Most businesses will have some form of liability insurance when they come in contact with third parties either in their own premises or elsewhere. It's hard to imagine what someone could claim against you if you're simply on a viewing walking around an apartment, but that's not the point. If something happens, you want to know that you're protected. Therefore, I would recommend that your business obtains R2R-specific public liability insurance.

Professional Indemnity Insurance

When offering advice or offering a service to clients, professional indemnity insurance provides you with protection if you make a mistake and your client incurs a financial loss. This type of insurance may cover you for the compensation claims and legal costs involved with your company's protection.

This type of insurance is particularly important if you are selling financial investments, in our case, deal sourcing for investors. When you present an investment pack, you should be making it extremely clear that your investor needs to perform their own due diligence so the investment risk is ultimately on them, however, if your property doesn't perform as intended for any reason, lawyers may come knocking. You should never need to use this insurance, as you'll be presenting good quality investments to your clients, however, mistakes do happen and you should be prepared for these if they do.

Contents & Liability Insurance

Each serviced accommodation property will house thousands of pounds worth of furniture which is at risk of damage and even theft. Content insurance is recommended if you're installing your own furniture, but you can alternatively offer to cover the landlord's furniture as a deed of goodwill. Either way, you can purchase this insurance yearly on a property-by-property basis from a broker who is familiar with the Serviced Accommodation strategy.

A combination of specific contents insurance and liability insurance is also recommended if a guest becomes injured within a specific property and can prove it was the negligence of the operator. For example, let's say a previous guest has left a marble staircase soaking wet, and your property cleaner for whatever reason did not rectify the issue. Your next guest arrives and slips on the stairs, who is at fault? Who knows who the legal system would hold responsible, but your specific liability insurance should offer you protection.

Landlord Insurance

As a R2RSA operator, landlord insurance is not for you to undertake or carry out, however, I want to make clear that if you are going to operate within a landlord's property using the R2RSA strategy, 99% of the time you are going to void their landlord insurance policies. What grinds my gears is that R2RSA operators, trying to line their own pockets, will not inform the landlord about this, choosing to ignore it for fear they will lose the deal. It's very easy to say *"well, it's the landlord's responsibility to make sure his/her insurance policies apply to the company tenants he is allowing in his property blah blah blah"*, which technically is true. But in my eyes, by not pointing this out, you are being deceptive with your own best interests at heart and I'm sure most landlords would agree.

Other Insurances

As your business grows, you may want to take on various other insurance policies such as employers liability when bringing staff on board, or business building insurance if you decide to set up shop within a commercial building. However, for now, these are purely future actions.

Information Commissioner's Office (ICO)

As of the time of writing, businesses which process personal information must pay a data protection fee to the ICO unless they meet certain exemption requirements. The ICO covers various regulatory acts such as the Freedom of Information Act and the Data Protection Act. The ICO is a resolution platform concluding disputes but also has the power to enforce monetary fines for companies which blatantly fail to comply with the law. If you're processing customer information, particularly if you are sourcing investments or managing properties for others, then you will fall under the requirement to sign up with the ICO. You can find more information about the ICO at ico.org.uk. To apply for your ICO membership, simply visit the Information Commissioner's Office website and apply through their step-by-step application process.

Anti-Money Laundering

As of the time of writing, if your business falls under the category of a letting or estate agency, then you are required to have anti-money laundering (AML) checks performed by HMRC on your business. These checks are designed as a safeguard to prevent businesses from becoming involved with criminal activity through fraud and money laundering. Letting and estate agencies fall within the same category as financial service businesses, high-value dealers and solicitors to list a few. More information can be found at the Government website linked in the end of book resources. Again, it appears that we fall into this grey area of defining what an letting agent is and whether a sourcing company should fall into that category. When applying logic, deal sourcers and some management companies accept payments of high, one-off, sums similar to typical letting agencies, where these larger payments tend to attract money laundering and criminal activity.

Therefore, it makes sense for R2R businesses to have Anti-money laundering checks performed,

Understanding Local Law

Before setting up your own R2RSA properties, you need to understand local law in your chosen city to ensure you are not breaching any restrictions set by local councils. Some cities have laws in place which restrict your ability to operate short-term letting services in certain locations. You will commonly find that cities will "zone" specific areas using a coding system, where in those particular areas you may require a permit, planning permission or a licence to operate a short-term serviced accommodation property. This system is becoming ever more similar to Article 4 HMO restrictions, although, as of the time of writing there are far fewer regulations focusing specifically on short term lets, although this is slowly changing as short term lets are starting to overwhelm the market.

The AirBnB website has a useful article which briefly highlights restrictions in some cities throughout the United Kingdom, which can be found in the end of book resources. Whilst this is a useful introduction, it is your responsibility to check with the local authority if you have any doubts or questions. I would advise doing this before looking for properties in a certain area so that you know exactly where you can and can't operate. If you do find a property which is in a restricted area, you could go down the route of trying to persuade the landlord to apply for a licence from the council, however, this can be a timely process and I doubt a landlord will accept the loss of rental payments until the application is accepted, assuming it even gets accepted. However, if you happen to own a property in a restricted area of a desirable city, it may well be worth applying for a licence in the background as you have an opportunity to harness this lucrative strategy. If you're sourcing

R2RSA investments, and I feel this goes without saying but I'll say it anyway as I've seen it before, please don't find a property in a restricted area and simply try to sell it to a new R2RSA operator who doesn't know any better.

Setting up your Business Socials, Website, and Documentation

Once your business is set up, it's time to think about how you want your business to present itself to landlords, letting agents and investors. Depending on the strategy you are implementing, you may want to invest in advertisements for your business, so we will assess this in this section.

Your business and social media pages are most likely the first pages your potential clients will see. It's common practice for investors and R2RSA operators to use Facebook groups to communicate, present investments, ask questions and discuss opportunities with the group. Therefore, it's not a bad idea to smarten your page up by removing the more horrific photos/videos as well as adding some of your business branding. In addition, you can simply create a business page on Facebook which has various steps to populate business information, which will all be visible to potential clients. I won't go into all the specific data you need to input during the business page creation process as it's self-explanatory, but here is what I would recommend from the feedback I have had on my page.

- Have a clear, concise, description explaining what your company is about and what it does
- Have a cover photo which provides further information on your business activities and what you can offer a potential client

- Describe your services in the "services" section, allowing clients to understand what products and services you offer
- As you start to source or manage properties, chase reviews from clients or developers
- Post somewhat regularly about your services, successes and challenges

A great tool to use for creating logos and banners for your business page is Canva. Canva is a free service which allows you to create and edit various business documents with the option to export them in various formats for varying applications. If you want to use my Facebook business page @studleyproperties as an example, my logo, cover photo and the majority of my posts were made using Canva. Whilst there are plenty of social media platforms you can use, I'm not going to harp on about each of them as Facebook seems to be the central location where most investors, sourcers and management companies communicate. Set up business pages on the platforms where you feel you can maintain regular posts and interactions with your clients. If you are planning on sourcing or managing for clients, trust becomes a vital part of your customer relationships. This trust is developed by ultimately building rapport through discussions and face-to-face meetings; however, your first impression will come across in your online presence through your personal and business pages. The point is, don't underestimate the power of quality and regular online presence as it will present your company in a position of power and will increase your network if maintained.

What I would like to add is if you are looking to take on a similar strategy to myself (which is scenario 2 in the "Defining your Strategy" chapter) then don't feel the need to go crazy with your business advertising. I created these pages when I was sourcing properties regularly, but if you're to follow a hands-off approach, then there isn't a need to maintain a strong online presence.

What I would recommend for all R2RSA operators is a professional website. The rationale for this is to attract landlords/developers to your services, where having a centralised place to refer to which houses your mission, compliance, documentation and FAQs is a quick way to build their confidence in your company's competence. Investors may well visit your website for examples of previous work and information about your services, so it's best to provide information on your sourcing services also. For your website, I would recommend you produce some literature explaining your services for the following fundamental pages:

- A home/welcome page explaining high-level what your company does specifically, demonstrating your compliance details.
- A page for landlords explaining why your services can benefit them, who you would accommodate in your properties, and why your company is a trusted entity. You can provide examples of where you have met and exceeded landlord expectations.
- If you are sourcing, include a page for investors demonstrating what sourcing services you provide. Include any additional services such as property set-up or management support. You can offer examples of successfully sourced units on this page once achieved.
- If you are managing properties for clients, include a page for R2RSA operators explaining what management support you offer with examples of properties set up under your management once achieved.
- A contact us page, demonstrating contact details.
- An FAQ page, answering common objections to the strategy and how they are mitigated.

I would also suggest a pop-up on your website which allows users to join your mailing list, as I have found that potential investors who are interested in your services will sign up, so it's worth following up once you receive these requests. I made my website using Wix's online design tool, which was more painful than simply paying a small sum to a professional developer. You can always add more pages to your website if you think necessary but, presenting the information within the above list will represent all the necessary information for your future clients.

From a personal point of view, I have a problem with how most R2RSA businesses present themselves. What I mean by this is that their online presence in some cases was straight-up poor, but in other cases, the businesses came across as borderline "scammy", if that's a word you can visualise. This opinion originated as I would come across some outrageous claims on company websites like 400% returns for their investors or the ability to reduce a landlord's expenses by 35% in big bold letters, so I never really got on with most R2R online profiles. Therefore, I tried to present my R2RSA business in a more sophisticated manner. Admittedly, my socials aren't as punchy, so maybe I'm losing out there. I would personally rather be presented well, with genuine content, as opposed to blasting a client with unsustainable claims. Hardcore salesmen at this point will point out that I don't have the "ride-or-die" sales grit, which may be true, but it's just not my style to bullsh*t for attention. The greater point is, before making your website and social media branding, think about how you want your business to present itself, whether you agree with me or not, and create a design off the back of that keeping a consistent approach across your platforms.

I also maintain a suite of documents that I issue to landlords and developers which provide more detail about the business model and how we operate. Remember, you will come across plenty of landlords/developers who don't know what R2R is or how serviced accommodation works. If you can provide them with additional details and examples, this can further your chances of working with them greatly. Visit my Studley Properties website for an example of one of my downloadable documents for developers.

Chapter 6 – Building your R2RSA Portfolio

So by this point, you have your strategy nailed down, you have created your company, you have the relevant compliance and you have your socials/communication methods ready to distribute. The final piece of the puzzle is to action your strategy. This section will be relevant to all the strategies previously described in this book. Even if you aren't planning on, for example, sourcing I would still recommend reading that section to understand how I believe sourcers should be operating and what you need to look out for as an investor.

The Company Let Contract

When a landlord lets a property to a tenant for a period usually longer than 6 months, these types of tenancies shall typically be bound contractually using an Assured Shorthold Tenancy agreement (AST). The assured tenancies are governed by the Housing Acts, where the very first clause 1(1)(a) of the Housing Act 1988 Chapter 50 defines assured tenancies to be applicable if:

"the tenant or, as the case may be, each of the joint tenants is an individual"

In other words, the tenant has to be a person and not an artificial entity i.e. a company. Whilst companies can let properties for residential purposes i.e. to allow staff/directors to live in a property, where companies utilise properties to sublet to customers or for R2RSA purposes, a commercial contract needs to be used. These are known as company lets, corporate lets or commercial lets, all of which are interchangeable terms. On the face of it, it appears there are a few key differences between AST and Company Let contracts, the main one being that The Housing Act 1988 does not apply to company lets, where the rules under Common Law take precedence in the absence of the Housing Act. This means that clauses covering Section 21 and Section 8 evictions, for example, do not apply. Also, fair rent increases do not apply to company lets, so rental increases are unregulated for company applications. Therefore, company let contracts also need to specifically cover rental increases throughout the term, which shall be discussed and agreed upon with the landlord prior to signing.

These are the basics, however, if you wish to seek more information I would recommend finding a solicitor who has experience in drafting company let contracts. He/she will be able to explain the difference between the two tenancy types in a far greater depth than I can.

The critical takeaway you need to understand is that you, as a R2RSA operator, should not sign for a property under an AST contract. A company let contract should be used. Where can you find a company let contract? If you want absolute assurance that your contract is exactly what you need for your portfolio, you can pay a solicitor to draft one for you. Otherwise, I can offer a draft template of a company let contract in the end of book resources. To be clear, however, I am no solicitor and take no responsibility for its content, advising that you do not use this contract without having your solicitor review it first. Alternatively, I have seen a multitude of R2RSA operators offering to sell their contracts on Facebook groups, although I have no record of these being credible contracts. In some cases, you may not need your own contract as the letting agent will have their own. Do be careful to check its content and ensure it's suitable, as I have seen various agent derived company let contracts which don't include the basics such as term length and break clauses etc.

A company let contract will be broken down into various sections. I've seen a multitude of contracts, all with different content, but I'll summarise the fundamentals that you will want to see and agree with the landlord.

- An initial statement explaining that this is a company let and not an AST, excluding the Housing Act 1988.
- A section defining who the agreement is between i.e. the company's name, the landlord's name and the date. This may also include any details of a personal guarantor.
- Term of tenancy e.g. 6 months and the start and finish date of the tenancy.
- The cost of rent per calendar month, including any rent increase agreements.
- The agreed deposit is to be held by the landlord, including the terms associated with deductions.
- The obligations of the tenant i.e. the company. This section may go into some depth, explaining how rent is paid, maintaining the property's condition, insurance requirements, access for inspections, property usage requirements, utility payments and parking arrangements to list a few.
- The obligations of the landlord. This section may include allowing the tenant quiet enjoyment, repair obligations, consent to agree, head lease consents and safety adherence for example.
- A section defining how the agreement can be terminated by either party. This section may discuss breach of contract, vacancies, bankruptcy and any break clauses.
- A final signature page for both the tenant i.e. the company and the landlord.

These headings will cover most scenarios, but feel free to be flexible with a landlord if a particular clause is going to be an issue for them. For example, I've had landlords ask me to go into more detail on a clause covering damages due to company use, which was a fair request. Don't be afraid to tailor each agreement to each property if required, just remember not to undo any clauses which protect your rights.

Property Desirability

Although desirability is somewhat subjective, there are some core traits of a good quality serviced accommodation property which make it more desirable for guests. This will improve your reviews, nightly rates and occupancy rates. I've included this section here so that the information is fresh in your mind as you read through the next section relating to sourcing properties. This will ensure that you have the guests' best interests at the forefront of your mind when looking for R2RSA properties.

Property Quality

A property's aesthetics and presentation play a large part in its desirability. When you're setting up, you can stage a property to make it more attractive, however, the property itself can rarely be changed. Using the "you can't polish a turd" analogy wouldn't be correct, as you would be surprised how much polishing you can do with staging and professional photos. However, if the property fundamentals are poor, such as an awkward location, an unmodern kitchen or a grimy bathroom, then the property will be less attractive to prospective guests.

At the very least your property needs to be clean including a presentable, functional kitchen and wash area. I look for high-end properties, which have either been constructed or refurbished in the last 5 years. These types of properties earn the best reviews and highest nightly rates. Examples of a couple properties within my R2RSA portfolio are shown below.

Figure 2 – Example R2RSA Properties

I would always recommend indirectly protecting your bookings by acquiring good quality properties where possible, as these are the properties which will experience the highest levels of popularity. You don't have to follow suit, but I wanted to position my brand on the higher end of the market. You may find yourself in a position where you are keen to set up your first unit and get offered a property that is okay, but not great. This is exactly what happened to me. After months of searching, I finally found a property in a good location. When I viewed it, however, the entrance was messy, the property looked awful from the outside, and the kitchen was okay, but grimy, past the point of cleaning. The hardwood floor was heavily scratched, the paintwork was patchy and the tiles in the bathroom were broken. I'm sure the property would've worked financially, but it just didn't "pop" like those in the pictures above. It appeared how you would expect an R2RSA property to look after 6 years of heavy use, not one that had just come onto the market. The landlord wasn't willing to rectify the issues, so I ended up walking away. Would I have made money by utilising this property? Maybe. Did it reflect the standard I would expect from a property charged at the nightly rate in my financial analysis? No. That's why I walked away. Of course, lower-quality properties are reflected in their nightly rates, but the difference in rent between a low-quality property and a high-quality property isn't that much in most locations, maybe a £200 - £300 per month difference. The increase you can charge in your nightly rate by offering a high-quality property far outweighs the difference in rental demand from my experience.

Location

We have already touched on the risks of picking a less desirable location in Chapter 4. To summarise this again, generally, you want to pick a location for your R2RSA properties which will experience a variety of clients staying within your property. This includes corporate clients (contractors, air hostesses, hospital workers, teachers etc.) and domestic clients who are visiting the area for leisure. The name of the game, diversifying your bookings to protect you against seasonality price swings. Most large cities tick this box, where you will experience a variety of bookings. However, that doesn't necessarily mean any property within a city boundary is suitable, there are other factors to consider.

Some cities have experienced such an influx of serviced accommodation properties that they appear to be over-saturated. Oversaturation results in competition, which ultimately hinders your ability to charge high nightly rates. Birmingham, I believe, is a good example of this. As of the time of writing, according to booking.com and when filtering for "whole apartments" only, Leeds city centre has 73 apartments listed, Manchester city centre has 133, Nottingham city centre has 70 and Birmingham city centre has 516. I know plenty of R2RSA operators who are actively operating in Birmingham successfully, but I would recommend that if you are looking to pursue more saturated cities, look for properties with more desirable fundamentals i.e. has parking, is close to the city centre amenities, transport links and offers plenty of sleeping accommodation. Even if your city of choice isn't saturated, I would advise selecting properties which follow those principles anyway as generally, properties closer to city amenities experience higher occupancy and nightly rates.

On a micro-scale, consider the specific location within a city carefully. If you were to pay £100 per night to stay in a 3-bedroom house, would you want to be greeted by an upside-down trolley or an overturned bin outside your door? Would you want to be next door to a student house blasting music in the early hours? You obviously can't plan to mitigate every disruption that your guest may experience ahead of time, but I would suggest choosing a location which will minimise the disruption. I try to stay away from properties which are, for example, above takeaways, or in particularly bad areas which clearly aren't taken care of and/or experience a high crime rate. Don't get me wrong, especially now with the serviced accommodation market booming, you can set up in these areas and most likely still make money. But thinking long term, your reviews will likely not be overly impressive and, as the economy starts to slow down and saturation of serviced accommodation properties in the area increases, your profitability and desirability will be squeezed. I appreciate it's a pain, but to understand how a city feels, and more specifically a neighbourhood of that city, you need to visit it yourself. Alternatively, asking a trusted friend or another operator within the

Facebook groups who has experience with that local area is the next best option, followed by a desktop study using Google maps.

What desirable serviced accommodation properties offer

The amenities that you offer as part of your service will also have a great impact on your reviews and occupancy rates. I'd recommend that you visit AirBnB, search for any city and select a few properties with reviews over 4.8 out of 5 stars with super host status, taking cognizance of its amenity list. These properties will most likely highlight the essential amenities that are expected within a high-quality serviced accommodation property. Most amenities are expected, such as full kitchen appliances, washing machines, tumble dryers, hair dryers and TVs, for example. However, here are a few more amenities you can offer to really make your properties more desirable.

- Netflix or Disney Plus - Offering these services at your property aren't particularly expensive however they offer clear entertainment value which 9 times out of 10 guests will use and appreciate.
- Private Parking - As we all know, parking can be expensive, especially when utilising paid car parks for long-term parking. Make private parking integral to your search for R2RSA properties as this provides a massive benefit to each of your clients, allowing you to demand a higher nightly rate.
- High-speed internet - I'm not going to suggest you go ahead and install superfast fibre with 500MB download speeds for your property but installing an entry-level fibre package over a legacy copper connection will allow guests to have a much smoother internet experience.
- Sofa Beds - Adding sofa beds to your property increases the sleeping capacity, allowing bigger groups of guests to book your property. This allows you to enter a higher nightly rate price bracket, but you can position your properties' nightly

rate a bit less than that of a competitor who offers that sleeping capacity by default. Therefore, you can earn more, and guests willing to stay on a sofa bed can save costs - win-win! A quick comment on this though, I have heard of operators who have let a 1-bedroom apartment and installed 2 double beds in the bedroom and 2 sofa beds in the living room to absolutely squeeze the sleeping capacity to the maximum. Whilst this may work short term, please consider the properties neighbours and use common sense when applying sofa beds. Especially in apartments, having too many guests entering and exiting will undoubtedly raise complaints from residents.

- Outdoor space/balconies - Especially in city centres, if you can offer accommodation with outdoor space this adds a large "wow factor" to your property. Whether you can demand significantly higher nightly rates because of this is debatable, but it definitely will make your property more desirable, and you'll experience higher occupancy rates.

Property Type

Both houses and apartments offer different benefits to your end user. Apartments are typically closer to city centres, transport and amenities, whereas houses will often offer greater sleeping space, outdoor spaces and private parking. I wouldn't worry too much about property type as each can generate healthy cash flow but may attract slightly different markets. I have found that houses often cater best for groups of contractors looking for mass sleeping and parking, whereas smaller apartments cater for leisure and single corporate stays. My point is that there is a market for both, so I wouldn't exclude one or another in your search. If you perform your financial and statutory checks, and the property appears to be a good investment, go for it regardless of its type.

Furnishing

I can't stress this enough, but the aesthetic of your furnishing will be a significant factor as to whether your property gets strong or poor bookings. Whilst searching for a R2RSA property, if you acquire a property that is already furnished but the main sofa is, for example, a 1990s leather sofa with torn fabric and cracks, you really can't afford to keep this in the property. The same goes with all furniture - it really does make all the difference. If this is the case, you could either try to negotiate with the landlord for a reduced monthly rental figure and take the property on an unfurnished basis or discuss having the landlord store the furniture. Companies such as Aspire Furnishings or Fusion Furniture offer ready-made serviced accommodation furniture packs which you can choose, purchase and have installed for a reasonable cost. Companies like these offer various furniture packs of different styles and quality. You have a choice depending on who your target market is. Main furniture packs include lead items such as beds, wardrobes, sofa's, dining room tables, chairs etc. In addition to this, these companies also provide add on packs, usually labelled as Bathroom Packs, or Kitchen Packs for example. These include smaller, yet essential, furnishings such as kettles, irons, cutlery, soap dispensers, bathmats and just about everything you have within your own home. The lead and side packs usually get you approximately 90% furnished, where to finish the property, you may look for additional smart TV's, extra artwork, bed linen, or soft furnishings such as floor lamps, additional cushions etc. I shall provide a general furniture list within the end of book resources for you to use should you begin to set up properties. Whilst it may be tempting to reduce costs and maintain the existing furniture, if it's in poor condition, don't. If you go on AirBnB or Booking.com and look at the best-performing apartments, they simply do not have old, tattered furniture.

Finding R2RSA Properties

In this section, I will first assess the sourcing process as a whole to give you an overview and show you how to perform sourcing duties in a manner which is genuine, transparent, and fair. Subsequently I will review the reality of sourcing R2RSA properties for others and using 3rd party sourcers. I'll introduce this section by again stating that sourcing properties is not a complicated process. The process is in fact very simple, you only need time, a thick skin and a can-do attitude. A high-level overview of the sourcing process looks like this:

- Understanding your own, or your investors, investment requirements
- Use online platforms or physically attend letting agencies to find properties that suit those investment requirements
- Calculate the properties cash flow potential to predict if it will meet financial expectations
- Contact the landlord or letting agent to enquire and view the property
- Check the property passes all statutory checks for R2RSA use
- If accepted, confirm rent and deposit payments (through negotiation) and pay your holding deposit. This will allow reference checks, if applicable, to begin and you will secure the property
- Agree to the terms and sign the Company Let agreement.
- Setup, clean and stage the property, making your initial enquiries regarding utilities ready for R2RSA use

I want to go into these points in more detail and assess how each can be achieved individually.

Understanding Requirements

Before you start searching for properties, you need to know what to look for. This may seem obvious, but you would be surprised how many sourcers look for any property, anywhere, and put in no prior research as to whether that property meets an investors, or their own, requirements and whether it's even suitable for R2RSA. Therefore, I believe this stage is critical and will narrow down your search criteria significantly. Therefore, whether it's your own company or an investor's company, these are the details you need to know before starting to look for applicable properties.

Requirements List:

Full name:
Contact Number:
Company name:
Company Age:
Email address:
City/Location:
Distance to city centre:
Property Type (Apartment/House):
How many bedrooms:
Rental Budget:
Are you prepared to provide a personal guarantor?
Is parking a requirement?
Would you prefer a furnished or unfurnished property?
Do you want your inquiry to be direct to the landlord or via a letting agent?
What is your monthly return expectation?
Are you self-managing or do you need management support?
What funds do you have to invest?

If you, or an investor, were to fill in the above requirements list, then you will immediately have a good indication of what to look for and where to look. If you are sourcing for an investor, they will simply answer these questions. If you're sourcing for yourself, note down the answers to these questions where applicable so that you have your criteria down in black and white. Based on what I have described in the previous section, I imagine that you are most likely going to initiate your search by looking for absolutely perfect properties that meet all of your criteria. This is fine and natural, but I can guarantee that after a day you will be quickly humbled by the reality that you will have to compromise in some areas if you wish to get your R2RSA business off the ground. The larger point is that whilst your requirements list is a great place to start and offers guidance for your search, it should be treated as guidance only. You can be flexible, and often are forced to be. This isn't a problem, as long as the property still passes all its statutory and financial checks, which we will explore later in this section.

I'd like to raise a few red flags that you can look out for if you do get responses from investors to these requirements.

Red flag 1 - When you ask for a rental budget, you need to bear in mind that an investor's rental budget will be limited by either their company's income or their personal income if they are acting as a personal guarantor. Anyone can say that their rental budget is £2000 per month, but they may not understand how the referencing process works especially if they are new to the strategy. The company or the personal guarantor(s) will generally need to earn at least 30 times the monthly rent annually to pass most referencing requirements, which in this scenario would be £60,000 per annum. I appreciate it's sensitive, but it's always a good idea to discuss this with the investor and ask if their company's income or their personal income meets these requirements. We'll look at this in greater detail in the qualifying investors' section.

Red flag 2 - If the investor refuses to act as a personal guarantor, then to me this is a red flag and will be a barrier for most property applications as the majority of landlords will look for a personal guarantee along with a company let. If the investor has no personal accountability for the property, they will find it very easy just to abandon the property or take little care of its condition. If the investor has an established company (3 years +) with a financial history and submitted accounts, these companies may not need to submit a personal guarantor with their application. This comes down to the reference company's discretion so I advise asking the letting agent or the landlord what referencing requirements they are looking for on a case-by-case basis.

Red flag 3 - If the investor has a monthly return expectation of £1000 or more, especially for a fully managed unit, and they are fully committed to this, then I wouldn't bother sourcing for them. To be clear, there are properties which will and can return £1000 per month but in most cases, it will not be consistent. Some larger properties may generate this income on a more regular basis, but the referencing requirements to actually secure a property like this are significant. If your investor can only afford a 2-bedroom apartment (I.e. their income is only sufficient to apply and have referencing accepted for a rental property with a maximum rent of £1000 PCM, for example) but they are expecting to earn £1200 per month regularly, I suggest they need a reality check. From my experience, I have found that investors expecting unreasonably large returns are often dreamers and will not purchase investments opportunities from you.

The Search for Properties

Now we have our investment criteria, we have a clear path to start our search. There are different approaches to searching for R2RSA investments, each with varying benefits and time requirements. As you make more and more inquiries, you will soon realise that you will struggle to recollect which properties you enquired about and when you enquired, due to the large volume of calls that you will be making. Once you have completed this book, I will offer a copy of my contact log so that you can easily maintain a log of your enquiries.

Letting Agents

As you would imagine most properties that come onto the letting market are introduced by letting agencies via their partnered online letting advertisement websites. Landlords looking for a hands-off experience will work with letting agencies as they, for a fee, will market the property, find a tenant, accompany tenants to viewings, perform the necessary reference checks on the tenant and action the legal documentation once a suitable tenant has been found. You will find almost all letting agents list properties on the following websites:

- Rightmove
- Zoopla
- OntheMarket

Through these websites, you have two methods of contacting most agencies. You can either call or leave a written message via the platform which transposes your enquiry into an email to the agent. As I mentioned earlier in the book, since I am full-time employed, I have spent a lot of time enquiring about properties on these websites via the messaging function on a morning and evening. To save you the same time I will openly admit that in 18 months I have not secured a single R2RSA property through this messaging service. Not once! Despite this being somewhat tragic, it did teach me a valuable lesson. Where possible, you can't beat a phone call or even better, a face-to-face meeting. I can honestly report that I have tried all tactics: short and snappy, extensive and detailed and everything in between. In my defence, we are in a time where rental demand is high so letting agents do not need to trawl through written enquiries when they have 30+ people on the phone looking to acquire the same property.

I'm not going to explain how to use these online letting websites as they are self-explanatory. Filter your requirements in the pre-search menu and it will show you the current properties available to let. What I will mention, however, is that Rightmove has a "Add keyword" function. If you type in "Company Let" or "Corporate Let" into this function, the properties that include this phrase in the description will be presented first. Occasionally you will come across a property which has "ideal for company lets" or something similar in the description. At least you know in this circumstance that the letting agent will be open to your business model.

D2L (Direct to Landlord)

Direct to Landlord enquiries are slightly different. Instead of communicating with a 3rd party agent working on behalf of the landlord, you will work with the landlord themself. As of 2015, Homelet reported that 87% of landlords used letting agencies for their property management. As landlord taxation and expenditure continue to increase, the number of landlords using letting agencies is decreasing as unnecessary costs appear to be becoming streamlined. The net result of this is that an increase in direct-to-landlord enquiries over the coming years is likely, so we need to know how and where to contact landlords directly. From my experience, when working with a landlord directly, the process of acquisition is much simpler. Generally speaking, landlords are less likely to reference you or your business. Whether this is a good or bad thing is debatable, but most importantly from my experience landlords are more receptive to the R2RSA strategy than most letting agents are.

You will find direct-to-landlord enquiries for properties on the following websites:

- OpenRent
- Gumtree

- Facebook Marketplace

As of the time of writing, these platforms offer far less stock than the traditional letting websites like Rightmove or Zoopla. OpenRent gives you the most probable outcome as it's specifically designed for landlords to advertise their rental properties directly. You can either leave a recorded voice message or a written message for landlords on the OpenRent platform, of which I have had success with both methods. One word of warning – try to avoid spam messaging large number of landlords on OpenRent. The website must have an internal system which blocks all of your messages to landlords after you have sent a certain number of enquiries. I have had this happen to myself, and the worst part is, you receive absolutely no communication or warning from OpenRent. All of a sudden you simply won't receive responses from landlords, but it's hard to tell if your messages aren't going through or if you have been blocked.

Gumtree and Facebook Marketplaces are multifunctional marketplaces which have the option to list rental properties. These websites are far less user-friendly, however, you can find a diamond in the rough. A quick tip for you. If you see a property on either of these two platforms and it's immaculate, it's most likely a scam post. Some people list immaculate properties at reduced rental figures, intending to scam users out of a few hundred pounds to secure a viewing. Don't pay any money to anyone upfront until you have viewed a property and solidified its legitimacy.

Developers

Finding a developer who is open to letting their properties to a R2RSA operator is rare. However, when you do find a developer they will often provide you with excellent, new to market, opportunities to which alternative R2RSA companies will have little access too. Developers understand that all stakeholders in a transaction are striving to generate income, which is apparent as you pitch your business operation to them as they can be far more receptive. Don't get me wrong, most will decline your offer similar to a typical landlord or letting agency, however generally speaking developers are less offended by the fact that you are wanting to secure their units for financial gain. As with all enquiries, some developers will be receptive, others won't, but it's always worth explaining your business, whilst showing them what financial and convenience benefits you can bring to the table when letting their units. For example, one of my properties is within a new development, where collectively myself and a few other operators offered to take on 5 apartments for serviced accommodation use. We even offered rent which was slightly higher than the market rate, so the developer was incentivized to work with us. The key to working well with developers is to create a "win-win" scenario for both parties, even if this slightly reduces your monthly income.

Finding developers is difficult. I'm not suggesting that you contact a large developer like Linden Homes and offer your services; they will tell you where to stick it within approximately 10 seconds. Small local architectural developers offer a much better chance of success. When driving within an area, you will often see scaffolding around a project with the developer's name advertised on the building facade. This is a good place to start. Of course, you can take to google and start looking for developers, but I have found that if you come across a building under construction with the developer's details advertised, you can enquire and be very specific about your intentions rather than just generally cold calling offering your services.

Financial Analysis & ROI

So, at this point, you probably have some tabs open on your computer with a selection of properties that you have found using online platforms (Rightmove, OpenRent etc.) that meet some or all of your criteria. Now you need to perform a financial assessment to determine if these properties will generate profit before calling the letting agent or landlord and making an enquiry. Over time, you will naturally know if a property is financially viable as you get to know the nightly rates and rental demand of an area as an almost sixth sense due to the months of research you're about to put in. As you become more experienced, you won't have to perform this step in nearly as much detail before calling a letting agent or landlord. However, if you are new to the strategy, I would suggest running the numbers first to make sure the property is actually feasible prior to wasting both yours and the letting agent's time.

To determine profitability, we need to dive deeper than the simple equation I discussed in the introduction. There are multiple factors contributing to the income generated. Below is a selection of equations which can help produce a prediction of a property's performance. One thing I want to make very clear is that although these equations do produce a reasonable profitability estimate, you will never be able to use this method, or any method for that matter, to predict exactly how much profit your property will generate each month. For example, different platforms have different booking commission structures, cleaning fees vary depending on the area, nightly rates change, rent and bills will move with inflation and the big one, bookings/occupancy rates fluctuate. There are too many moving parts to get a definitive answer, however, using this tool will get you much closer than most basic profit-predicting methods.

Before we start, I do want to clarify some terms that you may not be familiar with which will crop up in these equations. I would define the nightly rate as the sum of money charged to a guest for one night's accommodation, excluding cleaning fees and service charge fees. These fees are considered externally in the equations. As you would expect, different properties demand varying nightly rates depending on their desirability. I would define occupancy rates as the rate, or percentage of nights, of which a property is occupied usually within a month. The industry 'standard' occupancy rate considered by most R2RSA operators is 70%. In other words, in most locations, we would expect most properties operating as serviced accommodation to average 21 nights booked in a 30-day month. Some locations will experience higher occupancy, others will experience lower occupancy. I will explain how we can determine these factors later in this chapter.

EQ1. *Revenue = (NR × D × OC) + (CL × D/MN × OC)*

EQ2. *Revenue (Minus BC & CC) = Revenue - BC - CC*

EQ.3. *Profit (Before Management Costs) = Revenue (Minus BC & CC) - GMC*

EQ.4. *Management Charge = Revenue (Minus BC & CC) × MC*

EQ.5. *Profit (After Management Costs) = Profit (Before Management Costs) - Management Charge*

NR = Nightly Rate

D = Total days within a month (30 Typical)

OC = Occupancy Rate

CL = Cleaning Fee

MN = Minimum Night Stay

BC = Booking Commission (Revenue x Booking fee percentage)

CC = Cleaning Cost (CL x D / MN x OC)

GMC = General Monthly Cost (Rent,Gas,Electricity etc.)

MC = Management Costs (Percentage charged by management)

Starting with EQ1, we are looking to understand the total revenue produced by a property. To achieve this, we are simply summing the total fees earned. In general, your property will earn fees through two main methods. Charging a nightly rate and charging a cleaning fee. You may earn some additional income through cancellation fees, however, this is unpredictable and therefore left out of this calculation. The income generated through your nightly rate is simply the money charged per night, multiplied by the number of nights booked in that month. The income generated by the cleaning fee depends on how many nights your clients stay within the property. The cleaning fee income is defined by the cleaning fee charged, multiplied by the number of cleans expected that month.

Example: Let's say your property will charge out for £100 per night on average, and we estimate your property will be booked at an occupancy rate of 70%. The cleaning fee to be charged is £40 per clean, and it's estimated that guests will be staying a minimum of 2 nights per booking. Using EQ1, revenue will be calculated as:

Revenue = (100 × 30 × 0.7) + (40 × 30/2 × 0.7)

Revenue = £2520pcm

Some operators won't charge a cleaning fee, so the latter part of EQ1 becomes mute. However, I would always recommend charging a cleaning fee to the guest. The calculated revenue figure now defines the total income earned by the property. The remaining equations will now deduct expenses until we are left with a profitability figure.

The rationale for EQ2 is to determine what sum your management company, assuming you aren't managing yourself, will calculate their fee from. Cleaning and booking fees will also be deducted within this equation. Different management companies may do this differently, so it's necessary to ask your selected management company a couple of questions. The first is, what percentage do they charge and does that include VAT. Secondly, you want to know what sum they calculate their percentage from. Let me explain with an example. If a management company were to charge a management fee of 15% of your property's revenue, using £2520 from above, the management company would charge £504 that month. What I have found is that most management companies will deduct Booking Commissions (BC) & Cleaning Costs (CC) before applying their percentage. So for example purposes, let's say your booking commissions are 14% (£2520 * 0.14 = £352.8), and your cleaning costs that month are £420 (40 x 30 / 2 x 0.7), then we have a total deduction of £772.8. Therefore, to calculate EQ2.

Revenue (Minus BC & CC) = 2520 - 352.80 - (40 × 30/2 × 0.7)

Revenue (Minus BC & CC) = 2520 - 352.80 − 420

Revenue (Minus BC & CC) = £1747.20pcm

Now if we apply the management company's 15% fee to £1747.2, then the management company would charge £262.08, which is the process described in EQ4.

Management Charge = 1747.20 × 0.14

Management Charge = £262.08pcm

Therefore, EQ4 gives you the true management costs should you have your property managed for you. As you can see, the result is significantly different to the previous management cost estimate, therefore, it's important to understand what deductions a management company will make before charging their percentage fee. Depending on their answer, you may have to modify EQ2. If you are managing your own properties, the result of EQ4 will be zero. In your case, continue to calculate EQ2 as you need to deduct cleaning costs and booking fees from your revenue.

EQ3 allows you to calculate your pre-management cost profit. In EQ2, we have already deducted booking commissions and cleaning fees, therefore we now need to simply subtract all other general property costs. These include the following as a minimum;

- Rent - Agree with the landlord and or letting agent
- Electricity & gas (see below)
- Water (see below)
- Broadband – Use Comparethemarket to search for various broadband quotes based on your property's location
- TV licence – Online payment for TV licencing
- Council tax - Using the postcode and property number, search for the council tax band using the local council's website. Then, using the council's website, find the annual council tax cost for that bracket and divide it by 12 to get a monthly cost.
- Replenishments - This depends on the property type/size. A reasonable range from £25 PCM to £70 PCM could be considered.
- Maintenance costs - Budgeting £30 to £50 per month will often build a small kitty in the event you need to replace a TV or other furniture.

Further optional costs may include

- Netflix subscriptions – Online payment through Netflix
- Gardening - Get an online quote from a local gardening service
- Keynest (lock security service) - Get an online quote from Keynest.
- Furniture leases - Get an online quote from a furniture supplier

This calculator is only as accurate as the data that's inputted, so do your best to input accurate data to enter into these equations through agreed figures and quotations. As of the time of writing, I cannot advise on general costs for water and energy prices as supply chains are causing significant price fluctuations across multiple industries. There are some online energy price estimators such as Selectra but I cannot validate their accuracy during these times. For this example, I will assume that all the general monthly costs (GMC) sum to £1000. Therefore, using equation 3:

Profit (Before Management Costs) = 1747.20 – 1000

Profit (Before Management Costs) = 747.20pcm

For EQ5, to determine profit after management costs, we simply deduct the management fee (calculated from EQ4) from the profit before management. If you're managing your properties, you will have no fee to deduct here.

Profit (After Management Costs) = 747.20 – 262.08

Profit (After Management Costs) = £485.12pcm

And there you have it - a projected monthly profit calculation for a fully managed service. If you were to self-manage, you simply skip EQ5, where you will earn the full £747.20pcm as you will have no management company to pay. However, you will most likely have some minor fees to pay for a subscription to channel management services, which I'll explain later in this book.

The numbers I have used in the above example are close to reality, therefore I'm presenting here the real potential of how R2RSA can generate additional cashflow each month. I want to quickly review how lucrative this method, income Method 1 Chapter 3, can be should you look to pursue it within your business. As you start to scale your business, adding more properties to your portfolio, it's easy to see how you can completely replace your income through this strategy. Let's imagine you have six of these properties. I've selected six as an initial number because, assuming you have the capital to set up, there are plenty of sourcers offering great opportunities throughout the UK. Assuming you have done your own financial and statutory checks on each investment presented and they pass, acquiring six properties over the course of six to twelve months is entirely achievable. If you were able to self-manage your investments, I calculate from the example above a projected £4483.20pcm (£747.20 x 6) turnover within your business. Do bear in mind, your monthly income will not be this stable every month. Occupancy rates and nightly rates will fluctuate throughout the year, nevertheless, this calculation represents a year-round average monthly income. Your real monthly returns will follow a more sinusoidal relationship through the seasons, opposed to being linear returns month in and month out. I appreciate there are tax implications to consider, and you will also require the start-up capital to set each property up, but you genuinely have the power to leave employment with this type of income in a relatively short period of time should you wish to do so. Large R2RSA businesses have done exactly this, taking on twenty, thirty or even forty properties within their portfolio, bringing on staff within the business to support with property management. I personally am happy to limit R2RSA to a supplementary income method in conjunction with my employment income, however, I can see why others utilise it to leave employment they do not feel passionate about nor enjoy.

EQ.6. *Return on Investment = (Yearly Profit / Set up Costs) × 100*

EQ.7. *Payback Period (Years) = Set up Costs / Yearly Profit*

EQ6 & EQ7 are also useful equations for determining your return on investment and payback period. These two equations are the most relevant as they compare apples with apples demonstrating how good your investment is in terms of how quickly you can recoup your initial investment. To continue with the example above, I will assume that this property cost £6350 to set up, made up of the various set up costs defined within Table 2, Chapter 3. I will also assume that we are looking for a managed service, so I will use the "Profit (After Management Costs)" as our monthly profit figure, which we shall multiply by 12 to calculate the yearly income generated (£485.12 x 12 = £5821.44). Using EQ6, we can calculate ROI by:

Return on Investment = (5821.44 / 6350) × 100

Return on Investment = 91.68%

Using EQ7, we can then determine our payback period.

Payback Period (Years) = 6350 / 5821.44

Payback Period (Years) = 1.091 years

I want to touch on a few tips associated with reducing your upfront capital requirements, and therefore increasing your ROI. I've already mentioned that by self-sourcing and setting the property up yourself, you can save approximately £2500 - £3500 in set up fees. However, you can also reduce your upfront furniture costs by choosing to lease your furniture, rather than buying it. Instead of paying, for example, £3000 up front for furniture, you can agree to pay a monthly repayment figure over a 3-year term. Assuming your property cashflow's a healthy amount each month, then the property will pay for its own furniture. I can't exactly define how much your monthly repayment figure will cost, as this depends on the interest rate charged and upfront cost of the furniture selected, but I can advise that for a furniture cost of £5600, I was recently quoted a repayment figure of £230pcm over a three-year term. Obviously, the furniture company is earning interest off your payments, but if this reduces your upfront payment considerably, and you are confident that the property can still generate healthy cashflow after deducting the £230pcm, then you can see why this is an attractive option. If you sourced and set up a property yourself and decided to lease the furniture, then you could reduce your set up costs by around £7000 - £8000 in this example. This clearly is significant and will reduce your set up costs to paying your deposit, first month's rent, insurance and a few other minor expenditures. Let's apply this to the above example. I previously suggested that the set-up costs of the property were £6350. Let's assume £4000 of that is upfront furniture costs. Instead of paying that £4000, let's assume we agree a £190pcm repayment plan with a furniture supplier. This would reduce your upfront capital investment to £2350pcm, reducing your monthly cashflow to £295.12pcm (£485.12 - £190) or £3541.44 per annum. I can now run these numbers through the ROI and payback period equations as I did before:

Return on Investment = (3541.44 / 2350) × 100

Return on Investment = 150.7%

Payback Period (Years) = 2350 / 3541.44

Payback Period (Years) = 0.66 years

You can see how by leasing the furniture, even though the property is generating less cashflow per month, the ROI has gone up meaning you recoup your investment quicker. Whilst this is an option of which I know people do utilise, I personally don't. The reason for this is due to the break clause in the company let contract. Whilst all well and good on paper, what happens if your landlord decides to cancel the contract after 1 year by activating the break clause? What happens is that you have no income but are still required to make 24 months' worth of furniture payments. For me, it seems silly to take that risk, especially if you do have the capital available to purchase the furniture upfront. I personally see this as yet another way to make an already risky strategy riskier, but I thought I would highlight it in the event you are open to more borrowing in pursuit of higher returns. There is one additional major cost of which I have left out of this equation. Taxes. The amount of tax you need to pay is completely subjective, therefore it's a discussion with your accountant when your first year of trading comes to a close to determine your tax payment. In a nutshell however, your limited company will be required to pay corporation tax. On 23rd September 2022, the Government has announced that corporation tax is increasing from 19% to 25%, therefore you can expect to pay a quarter of your profits to the Government each year. If you're wanting to withdraw company funds to your personal account, you will then be liable to pay income tax, of which your rate will be determined by the income tax brackets defined on the Government website. Speaking with your accountant is the best way to become as tax efficient as possible, which is an absolute must over the long run. The reality is that you will also be able to write off some set-up expenses in your tax return, but your accountant will be able to advise where this is applicable. When reviewing our earlier example of acquiring six properties generating an income of £4483.20pcm, if we apply 25% corporation tax we can expect to achieve a post-tax income of £3362.40pcm, or £40348.80 annually, using this method alone. To achieve this, I would suggest you would need to be operating under "Scenario Four – Time Rich with Disposable Capital" from Chapter 3. Should you fall within the category "Scenario Two – Limited Time with Disposable Capital", like myself, then we can still pursue this method, we just need to calculate our income assuming we are paying for management support. Therefore, we calculate our income using the "Profit (After Management Costs)" figure.

Whilst all of the equations in this section are well and good, let's be honest, we don't all have time or a need to do manual calculations for each property we find. I'll make your life much easier by providing a spreadsheet within the end-of-book resources which automatically does all of these equations for you. To prove its validity, I've set the analyser up exactly how I have run through the manual calculations above. Now you can quickly analyse any property in the country to assess its financial feasibility, you just need to ensure the data you are inputting is correct and accurate. Most of the data can be obtained accurately through quotations or reasonable assumptions. Nightly rates and occupancy rates need to be determined through research, which I'll explain the methodology behind now.

Determining Nightly Rate and Occupancy Rates

Whether you are sourcing for yourself or investors, accurately understanding your nightly rate is critical to producing sound financial analysis. Similar to the comparison method used to evaluate a property's value, for me the most appropriate method of determining nightly rates is by assessing existing serviced accommodation properties in the area and positioning your property appropriately based on its desirability factors discussed earlier in Chapter 6. To summarise, these primarily include:

- Quality
- Location
- Property Type
- Amenities
- Furnishings
- Sleeping Capacity

I will first discuss manually assessing nightly rates as this is free to do for start-up operators. Subsequently, I'll discuss a paid service which can be used to validate the manual assessment. I want to caveat my manual calculations by stating that I'm purely sharing the method I use to determine nightly rates. I'm sure you could be even more thorough, but I'm also confident that you could be far less. I find the method I'm about to share a reasonable balance between accuracy and speed. Do remember you will be running a lot of these calculations, so speed is an important factor to consider. Feel free to adjust my methodology should you feel different.

In the deal analyser document that I mentioned earlier, I have added a tab called "Nightly Rate Analysis". You will see two tables, one for summer and one for winter analysis. The reason for this is because most serviced accommodation nightly rates are affected by seasonality, especially in more tourist-heavy and coastal locations. Therefore, to produce a more accurate average nightly rate for the year, we can assess both summer and winter nightly rates. We want to use online platforms to look for properties with similar desirability factors to the property we have sourced, using their nightly rate as a guide.

Let's look at an example. Let's say you have found a 2-bedroom apartment in the centre of Nottingham on Oxford Street and we want to determine its nightly rate. By following a step-by-step process, we can determine the nightly rate as described.

Step 1: Go to Airbnb and enter Nottingham in the location you have found as well as the number of guests it can accommodate. For the financial analysis of a 2-bedroom apartment, I would suggest selecting 4 guests, 2 per room. I appreciate that a sofa bed could increase the sleeping accommodation capacity, but the additional capacity, and therefore the additional income generated, will most likely not be utilised for every booking. Be conservative and assess your financials based on the property accommodating four guests. For summer conditions, select 5 weekdays for the check-in and out period during the summer months e.g. from the 22nd - 26th of August 2022. This will give us conservative weeknight rates for the financial model. The property will generate higher rates over the weekends, but again, we want to be conservative to not overestimate our calculations.

Step 2: Click search. You will see a map which shows various other properties listed on AirBnB in the geographical area selected. In our example case, we want to look for properties nearby (i.e. within a quarter of a mile or as close as possible) to Oxford Street. Using the more filters option, you can select parking, and the number of bedrooms and bathrooms to match that of the two-bedroom apartment that you have sourced.

Step 3: Using the images of the nearby comparable properties, find 5 properties which are similar in specification to the desirability factors of your sourced property. If your property needs some minor decoration and nice furnishing to enhance its standard, that's fine. Look for comparable properties which will match your finished product. If you can't find 5 properties, simply find as many as possible.

Step 4: For the 5 similar properties that are identified, select them individually and find out what nightly rate they charge. The total cost to the guest will usually be made up of three components.

1) The rate for the 4 nights (which needs to be divided by 4 to get the nightly rate)

2) The cleaning fee

3) The service charge

Add the nightly rate and cleaning fee to the "Nightly Rate Calculator - Summer", which is within the tab labelled "Nightly Rate Analysis" within the Financial Analysis spreadsheet shared in the end of book resources. Any service fee can be ignored, as we consider the service fee as the "Booking Fee" within our financial analysis calculations. Some properties may not be listed with a cleaning fee. Leave the cleaning fee blank in this scenario.

Step 5: The last row of the table will automatically calculate a suggested nightly rate for your property by averaging the nightly rate of the 5 properties found. By populating the rest of the table, you can check how similar the properties are to each other to make sure the nightly rates are suitable for the financial breakdown relating to your sourced property.

A quick tip. You will see some properties listed on AirBnB and other OTA platforms which seem very expensive. For example, you may find that two-bedroom properties in Nottingham achieve from £100 - £150 per night, but then another one is listed for £200 per night for no apparent reason. I would recommend clicking on this property in AirBnB and looking at its calendar to see how well its future bookings are performing. If it appears to have very few bookings in the future, this may indicate its priced above market rate and therefore should be excluded from your calculations aa an anomaly.

Step 6: Repeat the process, but select a 5-day working week in winter. Pull out the nightly rates for the properties listed and populate the "Night Rate Calculator - Winter". The spreadsheet will automatically average both the summer and winter nightly rates, giving you an annual average nightly rate estimate to populate your deal analyser with.

Step 7: If you wish, you can perform the same exercise on another platform such as Booking.com. This will give you another dataset to validate the information sourced from AirBnB.

Now we have this nightly rate, we can enter this into the deal analyser, along with the remainder of the property information, and we can see that it populates the automated "Financial Breakdown and Profit" table. The higher the profit, the better, but you want to be aiming for 100% ROI or higher on these investments. The property in the example represents a lower-end investment.

To finalise this section, I want to discuss AirDNA. AirDNA is a website that presents average occupancy rates and nightly rates for a given area. It is a paid service, however, it uses real booking data to determine these factors, rather than listing data from the study we have just performed. I'd like to highlight a couple of facts about AirDNA. The platform only has access to data from two booking platforms, AirBnB and Vrbo. They also partner with channel management services and Market Finder, which helps diversify their dataset. They may, however, miss a large quantity of data from Booking.com, which as of the time of writing, appears to drive most booking traffic to hosts. Nevertheless, AirDNA is a great tool to help predict occupancy rates and nightly rates accurately. Without a tool like AirDNA, you can't accurately predict occupancy rates. You will notice that the Deal Analyser will present Profit/Loss at all Occupancy levels in multiples of 10%. If AirDNA was to tell you that the average occupancy rate was 73% in Nottingham, for example, you could predict that your returns will land between the 70% & 80% profit prediction as an average across the year. If you want to be more precise, you could run a manual calculation on 73% exactly.

Contact the landlord or letting agent to enquire and view the property

Now that we have established a property is financially viable, we can contact either the landlord or the letting agent to enquire about the property.

Warning - this is the stage which makes or breaks a sourcer. You are about to go through literally hundreds of rejections. This is completely normal - keep at it and persevere

I thought I would throw that comment in there as it's true and can get very frustrating. As previously described, it's best to either call and discuss the property with the agent or physically meet the agent/landlord in person, as opposed to written communication.

I'm no salesman, quite the opposite actually, so I'm not going to go into depth about how to sell R2RSA to a landlord or letting agent as it wouldn't be genuine. Whilst making these calls, I would suggest presenting your services in a fashion which is quick and concise. Don't waste time, get to the point, and offer as many resources as possible to prove your credibility. Once you have one property within your portfolio, you can provide examples and financial breakdowns, showing where you have offered landlords more attractive returns compared to that of a standard assured shorthold tenancy. I also wouldn't mention Rent to Rent at all. I would use words such as "you are applying for a company let for serviced accommodation purposes". You'll still get rejected a lot, but most agents will go straight into defensive mode when they hear Rent to Rent.

One thing I will say, most R2RSA operators will go into calls with landlords or letting agents suggesting that they should pay LESS than the market rental value because a company let supposedly offers less hassle, less void periods blah blah blah. I honestly believe this way forward is dead. R2R & R2RSA operators have such little credibility as of the time of writing that I believe you need to be making higher-than-market-value offers to landlords to get their attention, assuming it's still financially viable for you to do so. Trust me, if you go onto property forums and look into landlords' opinions of company lets, 90% of the discussions are negative. The whole "we will provide you with a more hands-off service" is rarely the case and often company lets end up as nightmares for landlords. Therefore, I personally try to make it worth their time by compensating with higher rental payments. As previously described, each enquiry you make needs to be entered into the contact log so that you can keep track of your enquiries. This is shared in the end of book resources.

Checking the property passes all statutory checks for R2RSA use

Unfortunately for us, we can't simply set up a R2RSA property in any location or building. As a responsible sourcer, there are a series of statutory checks that should be performed to validate the use of a property for R2RSA purposes. Failure to comply with these requirements will most likely result in tenancies being cancelled early and financial loss for your business, or in more extreme cases, legal action.

Head Lease Compliance

Being non-compliant with a property's head lease is what trips most beginner R2RSA operators up. Most leasehold properties, usually an apartment within a complex, will generally sit under a building's head lease. A head lease is an overarching legal document which defines a set of contractual terms for all owners and tenants living within the building. The apartment landlord, or their tenant, is contractually responsible to oblige with the terms of the lease.

Head Leases are written in the language of solicitors and lawyers, so they are not always the easiest to interpret. A review of the head lease is necessary to find any clauses that either:

- Prohibit letting the property to a company
- Prohibit the property from being used as short-term accommodation

The problem you will have is actually getting a copy of the head lease to review. Always start by asking the letting agent for a copy, but from my experience, you will struggle to attain this document. If dealing with a landlord directly, you stand a better chance. If you can't acquire the head lease, the best you can do is get written confirmation from the letting agent or landlord that they have reviewed the head lease and are confident that you can operate within the property for serviced accommodation purposes. However, some letting agencies will say what you want to hear to get the deal done so I wouldn't trust this method. A much simpler method of achieving security is to receive written confirmation from the building management company themselves that you can operate the apartment as a short term let. At the very least I would expect a competent letting agent to be able to obtain the building management company's contact information.

Most poor quality sourcers will not perform this vital check. Landlords often won't even be aware that they could be breaking their lease, so they may not check. Negligent investors who are keen to get their business off the ground may not be aware or bothered to check. Finally, some of the less astute letting agents looking to secure their payment may not check. When these stars align, this is where problems occur. Let's assume that you have set up a property within an apartment block in breach of the head lease. Unfortunately, some guests will make excessive noise which may start to upset residents within the apartment complex. Normally this will lead to some form of complaint to the building management team. But there are other giveaways as well, the steel lock box for key access, the various cars using a particular allocated space and unknown faces within the building. All of these factors will, more often than not, lead to the building management company catching wind that the property is operating in breach of the head lease. I can guarantee the apartment operator will be out of the building in quick succession. There will be an absence of sympathy from my end regarding any financial loss incurred as it demonstrates a lack of due diligence - you have been warned! The solution to this is to acquire leasehold properties but confirm the head lease allows short-term accommodation. Alternatively, you could exclusively target freehold properties which have no such head lease. In this scenario, you and a landlord can do whatever you wish, subject to the terms of your company let agreement.

Mortgage Compliance

In the government survey *"English Private Landlord Survey 2018"*, it was reported that 55% of landlords use buy-to-let mortgages to fund their property portfolio making up 61% of all tenancies. Each of these mortgages has a set of defined terms issued by the lender that the landlord is legally required to comply with. Within these terms, often there will be clauses which prohibit letting the property to a company unless it houses core staff for a certain period of time. I have also seen clauses which say the property must be let on an assured short hold tenancy full stop, excluding any company let arrangement. If these clauses are present, and you were to proceed with a company let for serviced accommodation purposes, then the landlord will be in breach of their lender's terms which may result in disciplinary action. Ultimately, it is the landlord's responsibility to check these terms, however, I believe it's your responsibility to tell the landlord that they need to check for these specific clauses. As described earlier, it's good practice to explain these obligations to a landlord. Company lets are unique and have different considerations to a typical tenancy, which a typical landlord may not be aware of. If you're concerned about breaching mortgage terms, the solution to this is to seek landlords who have no mortgage. 39% of landlords as reported in 2018 are mortgage free, making up 30% of tenancies. The remainder of landlords are under non-traditional commercial, or family/friend, loans. This leaves just under a third of unmortgaged private landlords available.

Overall Compliance

To summarise, the path of least resistance and security is to find a freehold property owned by an unmortgaged landlord. Is this possible? Yes, but now you are narrowing your options down in a market where it is hard to find a quality R2RSA deal of any type, let alone within the confines of these specific requirements. Narrowing your options further, you have the local law restrictions which I will describe in more detail later in this book. The golden question is then, are all these R2RSA operators posting on social media operating in compliance with the restrictions listed above? **Most of the time, no!** Whilst people will happily post on social media about their large monthly gains, they won't post about their neglect, where their tenancy has been pulled from underneath them, or their investors, early. It's a common occurrence, and it's contributing to the bad name of R2R that currently exists. My advice is not to enter a contract unless the above compliance criteria are met. You will have investments fall through because of these checks, whereas others would secure them by being negligent. But when sh*t hits the fan, you won't be the one at a loss. Even if you want to take the risk, the landlord may not want to as it will most likely result in financial loss for them. With this in mind, your actions will not only affect you so be transparent with landlords about your intentions.

Securing the Property and Referencing

If you've got this far, the most painful parts of sourcing are behind you. The property you have sourced is financially sound and has passed the various statutory checks. Now it's time to secure and acquire. Securing the property is simple, where in most cases you will pay the letting agent, or potentially the landlord if working D2L, some kind of holding deposit which secures the property in your name whilst any referencing checks are performed by a referencing company. The sum of your holding deposit will usually get deducted from your first month's rent assuming you successfully secure the property, so I wouldn't consider this as an additional cost in your financial analysis. There may be some instances where you don't get referenced at all. Especially when working D2L, some landlords will find a tenant via personal interviews with candidates. If this is the case, great! Securing the property will be a quick and simple process with less hassle for yourself, however, in most cases referencing is common for company lets so be prepared to go through this process. The referencing process is fairly self-explanatory. The process may vary slightly depending on the referencing company, but in general, you will be sent a link to some kind of online portal with step-by-step instructions to follow. The referencing process will be slightly different depending on whether your company is being referenced or a personal guarantor is being referenced. If you're a beginner, then most likely you will be applying as a personal guarantor, so I'll cover that first. The referencing process will look at items such as your credit history, bank statements, residency details, employment history and identification. This process will flag up negative aspects of your financial history, such as County Court Judgments (CCJs) or missed debt payments. An affordability check will also be calculated. Remember what I mentioned at the start of the book, in general, the guarantor's yearly salary needs to exceed 30 times the rent. I.e. If you rent a property for £1000 PCM, then you'll typically need to earn a £30,000/year salary to pass the affordability check. Some reference companies will allow you to combine income with a partner to make the minimum income requirements. The system will produce a risk rating of some kind for you, and then the referencing company, corresponding with the letting agent or landlord, will determine if you're in a suitable position to accommodate the monthly debt. In short, if you have a strong credit score with a reasonable salary and no CCJs, you should pass through referencing with flying colours. However, if you have missed debt payments, poor credit history and a low-income relative to the rental requirement, you will most likely fail. In some cases, you do have the opportunity to apply again with another guarantor. This could come in the form of a family member or a close friend. If you're aware that you have a poor credit history, you should think about first clearing any negative debt (missed payments) before starting a new R2RSA enterprise. You may have already done this, however, nobody seems to know how credit reports work and I appreciate that negative report aspects do tend to linger on your report for some time even if rectified. So, if this is your situation, I would recommend finding a guarantor with a higher likelihood of passing on the first application to avoid failing and risking losing the property. Alternatively, you could pursue Method 2 (Managing) or Method 3 (Sourcing) as these income strategies do not require referencing as Method 1 (Operating your properties) does. I assume that the only person who would even consider being a personal guarantor on your behalf is a family member or a close friend, so please don't leave them with your debt if they accept and your property doesn't perform as planned. If your business is a few years old with some form of credit history and accounts, then your company may be in a position to afford the rent under its cash flow income rather than putting yourself down as a personal guarantor. In this case, your company will be referenced, where aspects of your business's profit and loss accounts, assets, loans, business activities and CCJ information will be reviewed instead of your personal income. Whilst this is preferred, companies are subject to affordability checks as well, so your company's income will need to be sufficient to cover the affordability criteria. Referencing isn't instant. I have had referencing results come back in 24 hours, and others in 12 days. There isn't much you can do during this process apart from getting your company let contract terms agreed upon with the landlord or letting agent, assuming they entertain these negotiations at this stage. You could also look at service suppliers ready for your application upon successful referencing.

I want to highlight a fact about referencing associated with the acquisition of multiple R2RSA properties. When you acquire your first R2RSA property, you have most likely achieved this by opting to be a personal guarantor for the business. In this case, the referencing company has checked your personal finances and deemed your income sufficient to pay the rental demand in the event that your company can not. Now let's imagine you are now acquiring your second property. As you are going through referencing as a personal guarantor, the referencing process will not, at the time of writing, highlight that you are already liable for the rental payments for your first R2RSA property. Assuming that your income is suitable to afford the rent of your second property, you will also pass this referencing process as well. Therefore, going back to our example earlier, let's assume you were to earn £30,000 per annum, allowing you to typically secure a property with a £1000pcm rental charge. Amazingly, or potentially devastatingly, as long as you go through a separate referencing process for each property, the referencing checks will allow you to acquire two, five or ten plus properties as it is not recognising that your liable for each of the other properties you are also a guarantor for. To me, this is the equivalent of leverage trading. You are still limited to the £1000pcm rent, but you can have as many properties in your portfolio with £1000pcm rental demand as you want. If all properties were to underperform simultaneously, your income would only be sufficient to cover one of the properties, not ten. Despite the obvious risk, this loophole is exploited by many R2RSA operators, who have leveraged 20 – 30 properties off a single income supply. If the referencing companies cotton on to this and begin to register other personal liabilities in the referencing process, then most R2RSA operators will only be able to afford one, maybe two properties, unless you have an extremely high salary in the late five or six figure range.

Signing the Contract

Once referencing is passed, you're ready to get the contract signed and start setting up your property. If you are using a copy of your own company let agreement, make sure the letting agent and landlord have seen a draft copy, preferably before you have paid the holding deposit, to ensure that the landlord is happy with the terms and you have had the time to negotiate any terms which require modification. By doing this, when it comes to signing the contract, the process should be much smoother.

If the letting agent has their own company let contract, ensure you have read all of it. Again, try to secure a draft contract so that you have time to review it thoroughly. You need to understand exactly what protection it gives you and under what terms you can operate and be removed from the property if the landlord so chooses. Don't be afraid to raise concerns with clauses if they are detrimental to your business.

A word of warning, I have had properties fall through at the last stage because letting agents have issued simply shocking Company Let Agreements. Some agents will literally delete "Assured Shorthold Tenancy" at the top of their typical AST contract and write "Company Let Agreement", which isn't suitable for a company tenancy. When questioned, they simply responded, "*this is our typical company let contract format and we are not willing to change it*". Now, if you're sourcing for yourself, you can decide whether to take the risk of signing up for an incorrect contract. I wouldn't, but you can. If things go south, it's on your head. However, if you're sourcing for an investor, please let them know of the situation and let them decide for themselves. Don't try to pull the wool over anyone's eyes. I have lost out on a £3000 sourcing fee because of this exact scenario so I'm speaking from experience. It was very frustrating, but the letting agent wouldn't budge, and the investor wasn't comfortable, so we passed on the property and all the effort up to that point was wasted. Just another day in the life of a sourcer I guess.

Agreeing on a start date is also critical for any tenancy. Setting up a property for R2RSA purposes takes time. You will need to acquire service providers, potentially a furniture supplier and have time to set the rooms up ready for guests. If possible, try to negotiate a 1 - 2-week grace period, which essentially means that your rental payments start 1-2 weeks into your lease. By doing this, you won't be paying rent for the set-up period. If the landlord or letting agent won't allow this, it would be wise to factor in a couple of weeks' loss of income into your financial projections. Most services you can get up and running relatively quickly. Even furniture companies can get to your property and install all furniture within a few days. One pain point you'll likely experience is that internet providers can often take a few weeks to get the internet installed and operational. If this is the case for you, you can buy a 4G dongle online with a prepaid SIM card which will allow guests to use internet services for the first week or two until the internet provider has installed their router.

Clean, Setup and Staging the Property

Contracts are signed, you've picked up the keys and you are standing in an empty property. All your furniture is on its way, so in the meantime, I'd recommend cleaning the property if necessary. The landlord may have already done this, but if not, a deep clean will make your property more presentable. Throughout this book, I have discussed the option of using furniture companies to buy or lease furniture packages which include the erection of the furniture itself. Whilst this is by far the most practical way of acquiring furniture, nothing is stopping you from going out and buying the furniture yourself. However, you will most likely spend more on items in retail shops such as Ikea and it is a lot more hassle, but feel free to get the experience. A copy of a typical furniture list will be provided within the end-of-book resources so that you can understand what furniture is required for a typical R2RSA property. Once your furniture is installed, staging the property includes adding attractive soft furnishings as well as additional extras so that the photos look as attractive as possible, ultimately increasing your booking occupancy. Soft furnishings include cushions, bedding and curtains, for example, contributing to the overall completeness of your property's high-quality look. The additional extras I spoke of include a bottle of champagne or fresh flowers put into the property for the photographer to again further enhance the aesthetic. Once the property is looking as presentable as possible, you can arrange for a professional photographer to take some photos ready for your listing. You also need to ensure you have your guest access method installed and ready at the property. This may either be via a wall-mounted lockbox or an online key-checking service such as KeyNest. I will discuss these options further in the management section. You may have noticed in my financial calculations I have included a management set-up fee. Some management companies will offer the set-up service as an add-on to their fee, so feel free to pass this stage on to a management company if you are short on time. If you are going down this route, do your best to coordinate access to the property as quickly as possible to avoid delays during the setup stage.

Now you're ready to list your property. Before you do, make sure any insurance, such as furniture contents insurance, has been taken out before the first guest checks in. Also note that for the listing of your property, I would recommend hiring a professional photographer with experience in property staging to take the photos of the property once it's ready for listing. This will position your property listing in the top percentile, making it more attractive to prospective guests. If you are self-managing, we will later look at the tools required to determine nightly rates through dynamic pricing software and listing your property on multiple OTA's using channel management software. You may come across a few spanners in the works throughout the process, but what I have explained is the general process from sourcing to listing a R2RSA property. If you're sourcing for an investor, the process is essentially the same. However, you are the facilitator of the transaction. Where the landlord has the letting agent coordinating for them, unless you are D2L, you are coordinating on behalf of your investor. You still go through the same process, however, there are a few additional steps associated with presenting your investment and finding investors in the first place, which I'll describe in the following section of the book. At the end of the process, the investor and their company will sign the company let contract and you will secure a sourcing fee, where past this point you will ultimately part ways until the next investment is presented. I'm going to describe the reality of sourcing for investors in the next section as it's quite a different experience to sourcing for yourself.

Sourcing for Investors

The reality of sourcing is by no means making two hours' worth of calls to then kick back by the pool for the remainder of the day. Due to glamourised marketing online, newcomers to the space do have a perception that sourcing is a method of earning quick money. This is due to the high value sourcing fee essentially earned via a phone call to a letting agent/landlord, which on the face of it gives the impression that sourcing is easy. However, perception is misleading. Sourcing can be a difficult task to perform correctly especially at the time of writing when the rental market is booming whilst R2RSA struggles to get credible traction. In this section I'll explain the additional aspects associated with sourcing for investors rather than for yourself, allowing you to make an informed decision as to whether this is an income stream you wish to pursue.

Finding & Qualifying Investors

The first step to sourcing for investors is having investors in place to source for. There is a common chicken and egg scenario which every sourcer faces. Do you:

a) Find investors first, understand their requirements, and then spend your time searching for properties which suit their requirements or;
b) Find a desirable property first which passes all financial and statutory checks, and then find an investor to purchase the investment from you.

I can fully understand why you would be tempted to get cracking and look for suitable properties first, however, I strongly advise against this. As I write this section, the booming rental market is causing desirable properties to go onto and come off of the rental market in hours. Renters are putting offers in without viewing properties. It's manic, but that's the state of the rental market right now. It will eventually cool, but I'm not personally counting on that any time soon. The point is, securing a property, and then spending the time trying to find the right investor will 99% of the time result in you losing the property to another party. You need to have an investor in place ready to acquire the moment you secure a viable property. Now that we have cleared that up, let's look into finding investors. The main channel for finding investors regularly purchasing R2RSA investments is again the Facebook groups. I've listed a few groups which are active as of the time of writing.

R2R Investments (SA/HMO)

BMV, SA, R2R, HMO, LO Deals & Success Mindset

Serviced Accommodation - Discussions - Deals-R2R And More

Rent 2 Rent Deals, SA and Lease Option Deals

Once you are in these groups, by using the search bar you can search for a location, say Manchester, and see all the posts in the past where sourcers have advertised investments in Manchester. The comments section will likely be full of individuals asking for further details on the investments. By doing this for a few locations, you will build up an investor list quickly, all of which will have similar interests, I.e. be looking for R2RSA properties in Manchester. Alternatively, you can start posting about your intentions to source in specific locations and see if anyone engages with you, however, these posts are quite common and from what I see investors won't engage on public posts unless there is an investment presented. When starting your property search, I would initially stick to only one or two cities first. Once you have a list of approximately 20 - 30 investors, you need to establish contact with them to discuss the requirements I presented earlier in this book. You want to understand exactly what type of property the investor is looking for and whether they raise any of the red flags that I previously discussed. After an initial message to make contact, I would try to initiate a call to go through each question in the requirements list, allowing you to initiate a relationship with the investor. It doesn't have to be longer than 10 minutes or so, but if your investor isn't willing to jump on a phone call, then from my experience they usually aren't that serious. Investors come from all levels of experience, some will waste your time, and others will be incredibly eager to acquire additional properties. It can be hard to gauge who is who, so here are a few points I look out for which have typically indicated that an investor is ready to invest.

- Understand if they operate any other R2RSA properties in their portfolio. If they do, this is a good start.
- Ask what funds they have available. Greater than £8000 will typically suggest that the investor has sufficient funds to set

up most R2RSA properties. Anything less than £5000 will restrict your search significantly.

- Ask them what type of property they are looking to acquire. If they are very specific, for example, "I want a 3-bedroom apartment in Manchester City Centre, within a 5-minute walk from town to a high standard" then this is a great sign as they have clearly put some thought into their decision making before your call. If they say "I'll take anything anywhere", from my experience, that's not the case and your search criteria will be far too broad.
- Ask them if they will be looking to self-manage their property. If they have experience managing, then they will have a good understanding of how the process works and won't be nervous to invest.

I'm not saying don't source for first-time investors as they make up a large proportion of the R2RSA investor market. However, be prepared to have to go through more turmoil to get that first investment sold as they will be understandably nervous and will often procrastinate. The likelihood is that out of your original list of 20 - 30 investors, 4 or 5 of them will actually respond to your messages. Let's say that you have discussed their requirements and I'll assume that they all have clear intentions as well as funds to get started. The ball is now in your court. The useful aspect of gathering various investors for one specific location is that you have multiple buyers for each property you have sourced. If you have one investor interested in that geographical location, you find them a property, and for whatever reason they don't want to move forward with it, you are stuck with an investment that you can't sell. It is important to have multiple investors with similar interests as it increases the chances of selling that investment significantly. Trust me, investors will drop a property for seemingly no reason, therefore I would strongly recommend that you have a few investors lined up. On the contrary, also be transparent with your investors. When you call to let them know you have found something suitable, mention that you have a few interested parties, so they need to review the investment pack as quickly as possible. If you want to search for properties in other geographical locations as well, follow the same process, and start to log which investors want to invest in each location.

On a side note, instead of calling investors via mobile phone, I would highly recommend zoom as a preferred option. I personally feel the ability to read body language through Zoom camera calls is a significant advantage and therefore is the option I default to. Utilising scheduling tools such as Calendly, you can pre-programme the time and date of your availability. Subsequently, you can send investors invitations to book a call with yourself at a time that suits them within the confines of the pre-programmed time and dates of your availability. Not only that, but the tool does give a professional impression and reminders for calls you have scheduled will come through via email to yourself and the investor. You can also add pre-qualifying questions to the booking, such as what funds they have available or what their portfolio size is, for example. This allows you to understand the investor's position before even speaking with them. Anyway, that's enough of a plug for Calendly, but you can find out more about their services at their website.

Protecting your Work

You may have been wondering up until this point why, once you find an investment for an investor, they don't simply call up the letting agent themselves and work with them directly. This would cut you out of the process and save the investor £2500 - £3000 in sourcing fees. Good question. The answer is, this happens all the time and there isn't anything you can do about it formally, however, I will give you some tips.

I want to quickly discuss non-disclosure agreements (NDAs) for a second. NDAs are common in the sourcing world of R2RSA, where sourcers will issue an NDA to an investor before sharing sensitive information about the property's location, letting agent or landlord. NDAs are supposed to provide a binding agreement between the stakeholders of confidentiality. However, in this industry, they aren't worth anything. An investor signs your NDA, receives the property information, and then asks their sister, for example, to call the agent and secure the property in another company name as a new enquiry. The investor tells you he/she is not interested and takes the property anyway. Unless you're a trained lawyer, I doubt you have the will or resources to build a case against the investor. You wouldn't even know it was their acquaintance that took the property. Also, in most cases, you will present the investment to a few investors, so you'll have no idea who has made the move on the property, so it is a waste of time from a protection point of view. However, aside from protection, NDAs will also list out a set of terms associated with any upfront fees paid by the client. For example, I have witnessed NDAs stating that once a sourcing fee is secured, should a property fall through due to an external party retracting from the investment (i.e. the landlord, letting agents etc.), then the sourcing company has the right to hold the sourcing fee for 3 weeks and search for a similar investment. I have also read NDAs that state if the investor retracts from the investment, then their sourcing fee is non-refundable. The point is, the NDA is a contract which can be utilised to define terms between a sourcer and an investor. This itself is a great protective tool for a sourcer if a debate were to arise during the property acquisition stage, of which you can refer to the signed NDA which will have defined terms before working together. Using an NDA, a sourcer can define their terms of service, and an investor doesn't have to sign it if they aren't comfortable with those terms. For this reason, if I do come across the rare investment I would happily sell to an investor, I do continue to issue NDAs, but I know full well it won't stop people trying to bypass my sourcing fee. I will provide an example NDA within the end-of-book resources. For me, building trust is far superior to sending pointless documents for signatures. Once you get to know investors, understand their history and get the chance to work with them, you will trust each other, and the process will become airtight over time as you build rapport. I don't know how to describe it, but I sometimes get a feeling when people are asking for details on a property as to whether they are genuine. Asking to have a zoom call, or meet in person, often helps distinguish the difference. It may sound silly, however, if someone is willing to physically meet you and show you their face, from experience they are less likely to screw you over. However, even then I have been wrong before.

To help avoid being cut out, try to attend the viewings with the investor and limit their direct communication with the landlord or letting agent. By keeping all communication through yourself, it reduces the chance of the investor having a separate discussion with the agent without your presence.

Pricing your Investments (Sourcing Fee)

I have referenced the term 'sourcing fee' throughout this book which is exactly what it says on the tin. Sourcers charge a sourcing fee in exchange for their time, expertise and finding good quality investments to be handed over to an investor. A typical R2RSA sourcing fee will range from £1500 - £3000, which admittedly sounds significant, however, there is good reasoning behind the cost.

If a sourcer could make one call, secure one property which passed all checks and sell it to an investor for £3000, then all sourcers would be very rich, very quickly. But this simply isn't the case. The £3000 also covers the time associated with literally hundreds of rejections, letting agents backing out, investors backing out, performing financial checks, producing investor packs, and problem-solving throughout each acquisition process. The point is, sourcers do work hard for their fee, but most are not ensuring the fundamental checks are being performed as discussed earlier.

Where do you position yourself in the market? If you are doing thorough financial and statutory checks on a property and ensuring its feasibility, you should be at the higher end of the sourcing fee bracket. The only exception is for small properties, usually 1-bedroom apartments. Because the cash flow of 1-bedroom apartments is limited, by adding a £3000 sourcing fee, the presented ROI to the investor is usually quite poor. If the property also requires upfront furnishing, then the set-up costs will often put investors off. As a general rule of thumb, your properties want to achieve 100% ROI or higher. If, for example, a 1-bedroom apartment is achieving 80% ROI with a £3000 sourcing fee, by reducing your sourcing fee to £2500 you will make your property far more attractive to investors. You can try to sell your investment at 80% ROI, just remember that you need to sell the investment quickly otherwise you may lose the property. From my experience, most investors won't entertain an ROI < 100%. The point is, feel free to be flexible with your sourcing fee. On the other hand, if you have secured a desirable property in a good location with a good pipeline of reliable investors, don't feel like you have to buckle to investor pressure to reduce your fee. If it's a good investment, it will sell.

Producing an Investor Pack

An investor pack is a document produced by a property sourcer which presents the essential information associated with a specific investment. Once a property has been found and checked by a sourcer, this is when they will produce an investor pack, ready to issue to their investors.

An example of a Studley Properties investor pack will be provided within the end-of-book resources. Below is a list of mandatory information which allows an investor to make an informed decision as to whether to add this investment to their portfolio.

- Key information about the property i.e. number of bedrooms, bathrooms, parking, furniture etc.
- A general overview of the property's location in relation to the area (don't give the specific location on this pack i.e. the address, as it increases the chances of an investor finding the property online and applying separately)
- Photos of the property's condition.
- Financial projections, including the total financial breakdown I discussed earlier in this book.
- Total set-up costs, including any deposits, sourcing fees, first month's rent, furniture, insurance etc.
- Evidence of nightly rate (snapshots from AirDNA, AirBnB or booking.com
- Contact details for yourself or a team member.

My advice would be that once you have produced an investor pack, instead of simply sending it out to anyone and everyone who wants it, try arranging a zoom call or face-to-face meetings to go through the pack with the investor. This way you can gauge investor interest and eliminate any concerns the investor has with the investment in real-time.

Selling your Investment

Once you have an investor on board, it's simply a case of your investor following the process within the "Securing the Property and Referencing" section which I described earlier. The difference is that you, the sourcer, will maintain the communication with the letting agent/landlord on the investor's behalf until the keys are handed over. The only remaining item for you to conclude is to secure your sourcing fee. This is a sensitive subject within the R2RSA industry. With so many scammers, investors are reluctant to hand over the sourcing fee until contracts are signed. However, if you wait until that stage, what stops an investor from simply not paying your sourcing fee? At this point, they are now in contract for the property, so if they don't pay you, they won't lose the property. It's a catch-22. I secure a sourcing fee upon application for a property. I.e. I provide evidence to an investor that I am moving forward with their application and request the sourcing fee as we are going through the process of referencing. However, I make it very clear that if the property falls through, for example, if they fail referencing, then their sourcing fee is fully refundable. I could show you bank statements where I have done this on multiple occasions. This has worked for me, but you could charge a small non-refundable deposit at the start of the process and claim the remainder of the sourcing fee upon completion. Any structure can work, as long as the investor is willing to play ball. There will always have to be an element of trust involved with these high-stake transactions, which is why it's important to establish relationships built on trust. I personally provide full refunds as properties can fall through at no fault of the investor; however, I can understand why you would want to secure a small non-refundable deposit as a lot of time is spent during the property acquisition stage and if the investor pulls out, I appreciate that you don't want to be left empty-handed after a considerable amount of work.

What you don't do is secure a sourcing fee before even starting to look for a property then drop off the face of the earth, scamming the investor and leaving them out of pocket. You also don't make fake investor packs which promise a great property and then scam an investor.

The process of payment is very simple. You will produce an invoice for the total sourcing fees due and issue it to your investor. Your investor will send the stated sourcing fee to your business account, via bank transfer or through a payment platform such as Stripe. To create an invoice, I would first recommend going into the settings of your banking application and seeing if it provides a function to issue invoices. My banking app Tide has this facility, so I can issue invoices directly from my Tide application without any third-party software. Alternatively, I can recommend Xero or Stripe as an online platform which allows you to create and issue invoices. Whilst you can trial Xero or Stripe for free initially, these are paid services so expect this to start costing you. I will finish this paragraph by explaining the feeling you get once you see that first sourcing fee land within your business account. In a word, elating. I was able to secure large fees, but provided a few investors with a compliant, suitable, and financially secure property in return. Knowing that I sourced a property and left no stone unturned, or clause unchecked, gives me peace of mind that I've performed the service correctly. The instantaneous fees earned allowed me to build capital to support with property acquisition and other investment strategies.

I want to review how lucrative sourcing, income Method 3 Chapter 3, can be for yourself and your business should you utilise this method as your primary income stream. Let's make the assumption that you can find, secure and sell two R2RSA investments to your investor base per month. Let's assume that you sell your investments for £2750 per month on average. Therefore, your companies turn over will be £5500 per month, or £66,000 annually. If we subtract cooperation tax, scheduled to increase to 25%, then this leaves your company with £49,500 per annum. From here, the most tax efficient method of extracting that cash from the business, should you wish to extract it, is down to your accountant to determine. Utilising the tax-free income allowance of £12570 and dividend tax free allowance of £2000, as of the time of writing, as well as the 8.75% basic dividend tax rate, you could expect to extract your cash with much less government expenditure compared to that of an employee paying 20% basic rate tax and national insurance contributions. I've used the example of two investment sales per month as this is achievable if you can focus your time into this method, and it can be seen how this has the potential to pay yourself the equivalent of a well-paid employee even in the early days of sourcing. This is just the start, you can scale your business from here, I'm simply demonstrating the entry level goals you can expect to achieve. To achieve this, I would suggest you would need to be operating under "Scenario Three – Time Rich with Limited Capital" from Chapter 3. Without being time rich, sourcing properties will become a difficult process.

Using Sourcers

Up until now, I have been giving examples and providing information from the perspective of the sourcer. What if you're using the income strategy of Method 1 (see chapter 3) and don't have sufficient time to source your own investments? In this case, you'll have to use a sourcer to find you a property that meets your investment requirements. I want to go over some common-sense tips to deploy when utilising other sourcers to mitigate the loss of time and capital through investments going sour. Whilst in some areas of this book I have been somewhat negative about R2RSA sourcers, there are some very good, legitimate sourcers in the space who can provide you with excellent investments. It's just a case of finding them. Before you start your search, produce a document which demonstrates your investment criteria. Provide details as to exactly what you are looking for, what funds you have available, your willingness to personal guarantor and what your maximum monthly rental figure is. By sending this to sourcers, I guarantee that you will be at the top end of their priority list as it shows that you are clear about your criteria and serious about acquisition, which is music to their ears.

Once you're in the Facebook groups, you will very quickly start to understand which individuals/businesses are regularly posting investment opportunities. Touch base with these individuals, send them your requirements and let them begin their search. In the meantime, feel free to look at previous posts they have made, look at who they have worked with and start asking people for reviews on their work. Word of mouth is always the best method of distinguishing who is reliable and who is rotten. It would also be wise to check their compliance documentation as this demonstrates their commitment to sourcing and legitimacy. Let's assume that you have touched base with a sourcer and after an undefined period of time they want to present you with an investment. Before you get stuck in, you need to understand the sourcers terms. This may well come in the form of an NDA agreement. If so, ensure that you read it thoroughly and ask any questions necessary before signing. For me, it's important to understand what their refund policies are should they receive your sourcing fee. If you're not comfortable with the answer, walk away. Should the sourcer have good reviews from previous customers, then you should be somewhat secure. If the sourcer doesn't provide any terms of service at all, then I would consider this a red flag. What if something goes wrong? What if they refuse a refund should the landlord drop the investment? I truly believe a credible sourcer will have a thorough set of service terms. Assuming you receive a set of terms you're happy to sign, this will release some form of investment pack from the sourcer to yourself. Irrelevant of the information provided within the investment pack, you need to perform your own due diligence to understand if the property is financially feasible. I would recommend performing your financial analysis using the spreadsheet I have provided in the end of book resources to determine how well you think the property will perform. If there is a major discrepancy between yours and the sourcers calculations, try to investigate what is causing it as potentially the sourcer, or even yourself has inputted incorrect or over-inflated information. A common trend is for sourcers to overinflate nightly rate figures to make their investments seem better than they are. Irrelevant of what nightly rate is presented to you, perform your own research and determine a conservative nightly rate figure for your calculations. You also want to see that the statutory checks have been assessed and confirmed in writing. Ask your sourcer to provide evidence, in the form of written confirmation, that the head lease and mortgage terms of the property allow for short-term stays if these restrictions apply to the property. If you have been presented with a mortgage-free, freehold property, then no such checks need to be performed. If these statutory checks are sufficiently evidenced, and your due diligence, in the form of financial analysis and occupancy analysis, proves the property will generate a strong ROI and regular bookings, then you are in a good position to proceed with the investment. A few words of warning, don't release any sourcing fee unless you have received confirmation that your business is going through the application process for the property. You want an invoice from the sourcing company for your records, with the sourcers company name and the sourcing fee amount. This is critical in the event you need to recover your sourcing fee should the investment go south. This should go without saying, but I would also recommend always viewing the property. The only exception is if you have a close friend, or sourcer, that you trust and has viewed the property giving it the all clear. Even this approach however should only be used if you are based in a location where it makes viewing that property incredibly inconvenient. Whilst this does increase your chances of securing the property, it is always a risk not seeing your investment and understanding the atmosphere within the locations itself.

Using Lead Generation

The purpose of a lead generation company is to provide the service of, you guessed it, generating leads for investors. In the context of R2RSA, a lead generator will cold call landlords with suitable properties on the rental market on behalf of your company, offering your R2RSA services.

On the face of it, this seems an attractive proposition as it reduces your personal workload if sourcing properties yourself. Adding to the good news, a lead generator will usually charge between £300 & £500 for their services, of which they will usually define how much time they will spend on your case generating leads, 10 hours for example. If a successful lead is found, then you have paid a fraction of the price compared to that of a sourced property. In that time, they may even find more than one lead which results in a successful acquisition, making them far more valuable than sourcers, right? Well, for me, this is where it starts to go downhill for lead generators. To be clear, I have used two separate lead generation companies in the past, so I'm simply recounting my experience here. The first issue to be aware of is that the definition of "lead" appears to be a grey area. To me, a good lead would be defined as *"a landlord who has a property on the rental market who is interested in accommodating a company let tenancy, and their property passes the financial and statutory checks discussed previously in this book".* However, it's clear that in general lead generators consider a lead *"a landlord who is willing to discuss R2RSA with you".* I do understand, for £300 to £500, you maybe can't expect a lead generator to perform full financial analysis, however, I do believe that if a lead is presented to you, it should at least be eligible for a company let tenancy through the statutory checks. This is simply not the case. I will give you an example. I had agreed with a particular lead generation company, before payment, that I'm only looking for leads which can legally house short-term accommodation clients. When I eventually had a lead presented to me, on the face of it the investment looked good. The property was a newly built apartment, and the landlord was keen to accommodate a company client. I found an investor for the property, who went through referencing and jumped through a series of hoops. During this process, I was pestering the letting agent to secure the head lease to review before the tenancy start date. Finally, a few days ahead of handover, we received the head lease and there were restrictions against short-term lets. When I questioned the lead generation company, they simply said that this form of property check was out of their scope, which maybe it is reflecting back, but the point is you may well be paying for a lead which in the long run will cause more financial pain through evictions. Another consideration is that the service payment is upfront. In other words, you pay their funds, then they start searching for leads. If they don't find any leads in their allotted time, then essentially, it's tough. I found that leads were being given to me, however, these were properties literally in the middle of nowhere, way outside of my investment criteria that I provided to the lead generation company upfront. To be frank, I didn't receive a single lead which matched my initial criteria, and the only one which was close didn't allow short-term lets. So, in summary, if you want to give lead generation a go, feel free, but I would strongly recommend not doing so if you are a beginner. If you do receive a lead you are happy with, then always perform the financial & statutory checks described earlier to ensure the lead is suitable. Never assume that, just because a company has presented the opportunity, it's viable for R2RSA.

The Sourcing Process Summary

As I draw this chapter to a close, I hope I have been able to give you a reasonable introduction to building your own R2RSA portfolio, highlighting the process and potential hurdles that you will have to overcome. Although potentially intimidating at first, the process is fairly simple, of which I'll briefly summarise again here in a step-by-step format to cement your understanding. I will assume that by this point, you have your strategy defined (Chapter 3) and your business set up and compliant (Chapter 5).

Sourcing R2RSA properties for your own portfolio, for the purposes of Income Method 1, Chapter 3:

1) Obtain any documentation you require for the acquisition of properties. This includes a company let contract, documentation referencing past successes, FAQs + responses, website etc.
2) Define and understand your investment criteria. This will include your preferences towards a property's location, quality, ROI, bedrooms, parking etc. Define your requirements using the list provided earlier in this chapter.
3) Using your investment criteria as a guide, start searching for properties which meet most of your criteria. You can search for properties via letting agencies, using websites such as Rightmove, OntheMarket or Zoopla. Alternatively, you can search for properties which are direct to landlord (D2L) using websites such as OpenRent, Facebook Marketplace or Gumtree.
4) Upon finding suitable properties, perform financial analysis using the guidance described earlier in this chapter and the Financial Analysis Spreadsheet provided in the end of book resources.
5) For the properties of which provide promising financial returns, defined as an ROI > 100%, contact the landlord or

letting agent to enquire and view the properties. Note that this is the stage where you will experience resistance from landlords and letting agents, so perseverance is key.

6) Upon the landlord or letting agent confirming that the property is suitable for a company let tenant, you need to check the property passes all statutory checks for R2RSA use. This includes headlease compliance if the property is a leasehold, mortgage compliance should the property be mortgaged and compliance with any local laws/restrictions.

7) Assuming the statutory checks pass, you can proceed with negotiating and confirming rental and deposit payments. Try to secure a 2-week grace period to cover the time required to set up the property. To secure the property, you may have to pay a holding deposit. This will allow reference checks, if applicable, to begin. Ensure you have a personal guarantor, financially viable to pass the referencing requirements, ready to begin the referencing process. At this point, discuss with the letting agent or landlord which company let contract they would like to use for the tenancy. If it's your contract, send a draft to the letting agent or landlord and ask them to confirm they are happy with the content. If the letting agent or landlord has their own contract, ask for a draft to review ahead of time so you have time to raise queries, if any.

8) Upon successful referencing, all parties can sign and complete the company let contract. Upon signing, order your internet/broadband package immediately to minimise disruption. You will most likely pay your first month's rent and deposit at this point.

9) If you are setting the property up yourself, you can go and pick up the property keys. At this point, arrange for furniture delivery and other services such as water, energy, TV licence and council tax. Supervise access to the property for the various stakeholders required. Confirm the property access

method via either lockboxes or keynest systems, which we will cover in the next chapter. If you are paying for a management company to set the property up on your behalf, pass the keys to the company representative and allow them to proceed with the property set up.

10) If you are self-managing the property, you will need to take professional photographs and list the property on the OTA's using channel management software, of which we'll cover in the next chapter. If you are having a management company manage the property on your behalf, simply leave the listing process to them.

Sourcing R2RSA properties on behalf of investors, for the purposes of Income Method 3, Chapter 3:

1) Obtain any documentation you require for sourcing properties. This includes a non-disclosure agreement, documentation referencing past successes, FAQ's + responses, website etc.

2) Find investors using the Facebook groups described earlier in this chapter. Look for investors with similar interests in terms of investment criteria, so that you have multiple buyers for each sourced property. Make contact with these investors via messenger.

3) Arrange a face-to-face meeting, or Zoom call, with investors to discuss their investment criteria. This will include their preferences towards a property's location, quality, ROI, bedrooms, parking etc. Send a follow up email confirming their investment requirements using the list provided earlier in this chapter. Qualify the investors ensuring they have sufficient capital for the set-up, income to cover personal guarantor requirements, and don't raise any of the red flags discussed earlier in this chapter. Ask your investors to sign

your non-disclosure agreement to confirm the terms of service.

4) Once you secure 4 or 5 qualified investors for one geographical location, use your investors' investment criteria as a guide, searching for properties which meet most of their criteria. You can search for properties via letting agencies, using websites such as Rightmove, OntheMarket or Zoopla. Alternatively, you can search for properties which are direct to landlord (D2L) using websites such as OpenRent, Facebook Marketplace or Gumtree.

5) Upon finding suitable properties, perform financial analysis using the guidance described earlier in this chapter and the Financial Analysis Spreadsheet provided in the end of book resources.

6) For the properties of which provide financial returns which meet your investors requirements, contact the landlord or letting agent to enquire about the property. Note that this is the stage where you will experience resistance from landlords and letting agents, so perseverance is key.

7) Upon the landlord or letting agent confirming that the property is suitable for a company let tenant, you need to check the property passes all statutory checks for R2RSA use. This includes headlease compliance if the property is a leasehold, mortgage compliance should the property be mortgaged and compliance with any local laws/restrictions.

8) Assuming the statutory checks pass, you can proceed with negotiating and confirming rental and deposit payments. Try to secure a 2-week grace period to cover the time required to set up the property.

9) Once these details are confirmed, you know the property is suitable to sell to an investor. Create an investor pack including details on the property, its financial projections, features and set up costs. Send your investors the

investment pack. Should an investor look to proceed with the investment, you will need to arrange a viewing for your investor to visit the property.

10) Should the investor wish to proceed, we can proceed to secure the property. Send an invoice to the investor including the sourcing fee as well as the holding fee, if applicable. Once you receive these funds, pay the holding fee, if applicable, to the letting agent or landlord. This will allow reference checks, if applicable, to begin. Ensure the investor has a personal guarantor, financially viable to pass the referencing requirements, ready to begin the referencing process. At this point, discuss with the letting agent or landlord which company let contract they would like to use for the tenancy. If it's your contract, send a draft to the letting agent or landlord and ask them to confirm they are happy with the content. If the letting agent or landlord has their own contract, ask for a draft for the investor to review ahead of time so they have time to raise queries, if any.

Upon successful referencing, all parties can sign and complete the company let contract. The investor will most likely pay their first month's rent and deposit at this point. Unless you are managing the property on the investor's behalf, this is the end of your sourcing process, where you allow the investor to pick up the keys and proceed with setup.

Should you be operating under Scenario 2 (Limited Time with Disposable Capital, Chapter 3) you may well be looking for sourcers to present investments to you. In this case, the above step by step processes are not applicable. You simply need to take any information presented by a sourcer and validate it using the financial analysis spreadsheet and confirming the statutory checks pass. If you are happy with the investment, you can proceed with sending the sourcer their sourcing fee and holding deposit to begin the referencing process. Follow the guidance within the "Using Sourcers" section of this chapter.

Chapter 7 – R2RSA Property Management

Now we have looked into acquiring properties, we need to understand the appropriate methods used for managing the investment. In this section, we'll review how to manage a R2RSA property for both your portfolio and other investors if you wish to expand your income through management services. Note that some of the upcoming sections will only be relevant if you are managing properties for clients. Even if you don't plan to, I still would give them a read so you know what to expect from your selected management company.

Before we look into the various aspects of property management, I wanted to start with the basics by reviewing the goals of a good management company. As a manager of short-term accommodation, what are you providing? I think it's important that it's understood that a management company is primarily providing a service for every guest that books your accommodation. Your guests are your priority, as these are the people who keep your somewhat risky investment strategy alive and profitable. Whilst this may seem obvious, I'm discussing this because from my experience start-up management companies often focus on maximising their profit as a priority, which is important, but don't attend to their guests' needs as attentively as they should. This ultimately leads to poor initial reviews and reduced bookings in that vital early stage of a property launch. Positive reviews, and quality listings, on common Online Travel Agencies (OTAs) such as AirBnB, Booking.com and Expedia are critical aspects involved with the listing/ranking algorithms. In simple terms, the higher the quality of your listing, the more eyes will see that listing.

In the past, I too have personally tried to squeeze my expenses to maximise profit, admittedly at the cost of my clients. It's human psychology, and only natural to minimise costs as much as possible. What you need to consider, however, is that for every decision you make which will impact a guest's experience, ask yourself, or even better an honest friend, how would that make you feel as a guest recipient. If you attended a property and the interior design was not coordinated and in a poor state, would you write a good review? If you messaged your host with a vital question about how to operate the central heating and you didn't receive a response for hours, would you write a good review? If you arrived at the property and the cleaners hadn't tidied the previous guests' mess, would you write a good review? These examples of deficient management styles may incur less cost for your company, but they will have an impact on your future profitability. Now let's flip the perspective. You attend a property and you're greeted with a list of the popular amenities (restaurants, local attractions, convenience stores etc.) with contact numbers in case of questions or emergencies, would this at the very least contribute to a good review? Yes! If you looked in the fridge and the host has stocked essentials such as bread, milk, butter etc. would this at the very least contribute to a good review? Absolutely. I think you get my point - small skimming of cost and service quality will reduce your profitability in the medium to long term and incurring small thoughtful costs to enhance guest experience will elevate your profitability in the medium to long term. To go full circle then, your primary goal is to provide the best service possible for your guests. This will ultimately improve your profitability. Your secondary goal then is to focus on receiving bookings at the highest occupancy rate possible, which can be achieved by acting proactively and harnessing tools to maximise your efficiency. By achieving the first and second goals above, you will not only be maximising your own profits, but also those of your investors, should you be managing on behalf of other businesses. This brings us onto your third priority, maintaining investor confidence in your performance, as well as maintaining profitability for investors. Keeping your investors happy will maintain your management income stream into the future, allowing your business to build strong cashflow. Now that we have assessed the goals of a management company, let's look at the various aspects which make up management operations.

The Management Contract

Whether you are utilising a management company for your portfolio, or you plan on managing a client's portfolio, you will at some stage be exposed to a management contract. A management contract simply defines all terms between an investor and their associated management company. Whilst contracts will come in different forms, the following list highlights common terms presented and agreed upon within typical management agreements.

- A list of the stakeholders involved in the contract, I.e. both the investors and the management company names, company numbers, representative names and the agreement start date.
- Initial headline agreement information such as the property address, monthly fee charged by the management company, expected payment date for-profit and running costs, the term length and any setup fees.
- A list of any rent reviews, break clauses, or specific/unique agreements with the landlord
- A list of the management companies' obligations.
- A list of the investors' obligations.
- A section defining contract termination procedures, such as bankruptcy or breach of contract.
- A list of terms associated with notices provided between stakeholders.

- General details around data protection, insurance requirements, governing laws etc.

Similar to the company let contract discussed earlier, whilst the above is a good starting point, most management companies will be somewhat flexible if you aren't comfortable with some of the defined terms. If you have been sent a management agreement that you're not happy with, don't be afraid to challenge the company and ask questions. If your business has issued a management contract and your investors have queries, feel free to be flexible as long as it doesn't put you or your company at risk. A typical management contract will be provided within the end-of-book resources.

If you're issuing management contracts to clients, I would recommend using online signature tools such as DocuSign or PandaDoc. These systems allow clients to sign PDF documents using legally binding e-signatures. The client receives an email with the contracts, signs the document on the chosen platform, and you're now in contract. It really is that simple. These tools save significant time posting and wet-signing documents for a low fee.

Using a Channel Manager

Within the accommodation industry, there are a variety of different Online Travel Agencies (OTAs) which make up the online booking market. The business model of these OTA's is simple, they connect guests with hosts, and charge a fee for doing so. I unfortunately don't have live data providing evidence as to which OTA's have what percentage of market share, but I can show you evidence as to what OTA's have been commonly used when booking one of my R2RSA units. The below ring chart demonstrates which OTA platforms have been used to book an apartment I'm operating over a timeframe of 6 months.

Stays between 12 Apr 2022 and 12 Oct 2022

Figure 3 – Example OTA Bookings

Frustratingly, I can't change the colours on the chart segments to make an obvious distinction, so to summarise: Booking.com (47%), AirBnB (30%), Phone/Direct Contact (17%), Expedia & Affiliate Network (5%) & Vrbo (1%). The apartment is subject to bookings from various OTA platforms, which traditionally was the root of various problems for property managers as these platforms did not exchange information between each other. For example, let's say you have an apartment listed on all the platforms above. If your apartment was booked for a week in July on AirBnB, that booking information would not be passed to your listing on Booking.com, therefore another guest might also book that week on Booking.com. Now you have a double booking, so you're going to have to cancel one of the two, subjecting you to potential cancellation fees. This is just one example, but generally having to manually correspond and alter your listings across various platforms is time-consuming, and often leads to human error. This is where a channel manager becomes extremely useful. A channel manager is an essential tool which is a single online platform which managers use to list, manage and control properties. The software integrates with the various OTA's and synchronises calendars and listing alterations across the platforms, meaning all OTA's present the same information across the board. This fact alone streamlines the management process tenfold. Should you be managing R2RSA properties on behalf of other companies using the Income Method 2 from Chapter 3, then you will need to utilise the reporting tool within your channel management software to print profit/loss reports for each investor. Where traditional property investors use manual KPIs to track performance, by using a channel manager you instantaneously have access to occupancy rates, revenue produced, average nightly rate, cancellation fee revenue, cleaning fee revenue, platform commission costs and so much more. If you're managing properties for other businesses, this is a quick and professional way of printing reports and sharing performance information. Your profit/loss reports allow you and the investor to visually see the financial performance. Similar to how I have presented in the financial analysis section, the reports will present the monthly gross income, and then subtract platform commissions, management fees, replenishment costs, cleaning fee's etc. presenting a net income produced by the property. This net income is then issued to the investor, with the profit/loss report to prove its validity. I will describe this concept with an example. Using the same figures from the financial analysis section example, the investors outgoings are represented as below:

Rent (Paid to the Landlord) = £650

Electricity/Gas (Paid to Energy Supplier) = £100

Water (Paid to Water Supplier) = £30

Netflix = £6

Council Tax (Paid to Council) = £114

Gardening Upkeep = £20

Minor Repairs = £30

Total = £970

Therefore, the investor has spent £970 this particular month to pay for the property's operation. Now let's say, for example, that the property generated £2794.20 that month in gross income. This income will be made up of various nightly rates, which will fluctuate throughout the month based on demand, as well as cleaning fees and your occupancy rate. Your channel management software will define the precise occupancy rate and average monthly nightly rate achieved. In your profit/loss report, you will be presented with all the deductions paid out of the property's gross income. This is where the reality of the property's income starts to differ from the financial analysis section described earlier. In the financial analysis section, we used average figures, such as predicted nightly rates, platform commissions equalling 14%, cleaning fees assumed to be once every two nights and replenishments equalling £30 per month. However, the reality of these figures will present a different picture. This month, platform commission fee's may be 15.6% for example, replenishments may be more than predicted, but you may have only had a cleaner in the property once every three nights, instead of two. Therefore, the deductions in the profit/loss report will most likely not match with your financial projections. For example purposes only, I have applied non calculated arbitrary deduction costs below.

Platform commission fee's = £386.48

Management fees = £271.20

Replenishment costs = £45

Cleaning fee's = £311.20

Total = £1013.88

Therefore, the net income to be issued to the investor after deductions is £1780.32 (£2794.20 gross income minus £1013.88 of deductions). Therefore, the investor spent £970, and received £1780.32 in the same month, creating a profit of £810.32 for that month. You can see here how the manual calculations produced earlier are a good guide, however don't provide fully accurate predictions as variations in the income effect the net payment to the investor. Whilst in this example, on this particular month, we have received stronger returns than expected, there will be other months that provide returns on the contrary. Thus, creating the variation in income that I've described throughout this book. The profit/loss report will clarify this point monthly, describing how the net payment to the investor has been derived.

Another benefit when utilising channel management software is that you have the ability to add guest viewers to a specific property, who can view live information such as upcoming bookings and performance. This is especially useful for sharing with your cleaners, who have live access to the property calendar. This allows your cleaning team to plan their workload around upcoming bookings within the property. Some channel managers can automate responses to guests upon booking through their respective platforms. This ability further improves customer interface whilst being highly efficient. You have the ability to write a polite welcome email as a template within the channel manager which will be issued to your guest without any interface from yourself. The above presents a few generic benefits of channel managers, however, I would highly recommend looking at the various websites to understand the specific benefits of the different platforms. A few examples of channel managers include:

- Eviivo
- Guesty
- Tokeet

These are all paid services, so feel free to investigate pricing and the benefits of each platform before selecting one in particular. The good news is that all three platforms listed above do offer a free trial to help inform your decision. If, like me, you use a management company to manage your properties for you, always check that they use a channel manager. This is more applicable for start-up management companies, as the last thing you want is to be paying for a poor management service which again, will lose you money in the medium to long term.

Setting Nightly Rates

If you have got to this stage where you have acquired a property and are ready to manage it, you should have a somewhat conservative idea of what average nightly rate your specific property can achieve throughout the working week from your financial analysis discussed earlier in this book. This will have been based on its quality, location, property type, amenities, furnishings and sleeping capacity. Whilst your calculations were based on approximately average, or slightly below for simplification purposes, true nightly rates are far from static throughout the year and even day to day. There are core aspects outside of the above which will increase your nightly rate, including:

- Local Events
- Weekend Rates
- Seasons
- Holiday Periods/Bank Holiday/New Year
- Single Night Stays

As we have all experienced when booking holidays or getaways, a substantial increase in the price of accommodation can be expected when your bookings co-inside with the list above. The channel management software discussed earlier recognises this, so it provides you with complete flexibility to edit your nightly rates daily to maximise profitability. I can't accurately advise what percentage increase in nightly rate you should apply during these periods. Your nightly rates will fluctuate based on a multitude of unknown factors to me, so you will have to perform some further location-specific research to understand where your property can fit in the market compared to other comparables. The nightly rate market does fluctuate fairly regularly based on supply and demand within the area, therefore it's worth at least reviewing your rates bi-weekly to ensure you're priced correctly against the competition. I want to briefly expand on single-night stays and why these increase your nightly rate. If you accommodate a different guest every night, compared to limiting guests to staying two nights as a minimum, you have immediately doubled your cleaning fee as your cleaners are attending the property twice as much. To mitigate this, it's common for managers to set a higher nightly rate for a single night stay to ensure their property is operating at the usual level of profitability. On the contrary, there may be times when you compromise on your nightly rate in pursuit of high occupancy and locking in bookings. These include:

- Offering an early bird discount to guests that book your accommodation in advance
- Offering reduced nightly rates for long-term bookings
- Offering non-refundable and refundable prices at different rates

The goal of using the above techniques is to incentivise guests to book your property in advance and for longer durations, which increases your occupancy rating. By deploying these strategies, you may be missing out on future bookings that could occupy your property at a higher nightly rate, but these bookings are not guaranteed. My advice would be to welcome long-term bookings but first, you need to assess how much of a discount is reasonable. To do this, you can use the deal analyser spreadsheet I'm going to provide you with within the end-of-book resources. Simply reduce your nightly rate, by say £5 per night, for the long-term booking. This obviously will reduce your income, but instead of looking at the typical 70% occupancy rate figure, look at the profitability of higher occupancy rates around 90%, or even 100% if it's a month-long booking. Depending on the nightly rate you agree with the long-term guest, you may even end up more profitable by using this strategy because of the higher occupancy rate. In a similar light, offering non-refundable rates is a good way of securing payment from a guest. Granted, it generates less profit, but it firmly ensures your guest can't cancel their booking, or if they do, they won't receive a refund. This removes some risk from you, the host, and cements occupancy rates. If all this price adjustment sounds tedious, I have a solution for you. Integrating with your channel manager, various automated software is available which will dynamically adjust your nightly rate based on the factors I discussed above. Example software includes:

- Beyond
- PriceLabs
- Wheelhouse

To utilise this type of software, you simply sign up, pay a small subscription fee and let the algorithms behind the software work their magic. You can control the algorithm to an extent by, for example, defining maximum and minimum price swings based on how aggressively you're prioritising occupancy. Based on your parameters, the software will use real-time data from competitors to price your property competitively. It goes without saying that this software will be a great tool when bringing efficiencies into your business. And yes, more good news, each of the above do provide free trials.

Payment Gateway Platform

A centralised payment platform used to accept payments is recommended as you start to scale and accept more payments within your R2RSA business. Especially with the payment exposure levels in our industry, you'll be experiencing high volumes of payments from credit cards, debit cards, apple pay, google pay and even foreign payment platforms via guests overseas. Therefore, it's important to have the infrastructure to accommodate these payments efficiently, contributing to the ease of experience for your accommodation guests. There are various financial services available dedicated to providing small businesses with payment assistance. Two platforms which offer suitable services for our industry include, but are not limited to:

- Stripe
- PayPal

I would immediately like to point out that whilst I've given two options above for the purposes of diversification, I truly believe that the former provides the best services for what we require when managing properties. From my experience, PayPal offers a secure, efficient payment platform for invoicing and receiving payments for a single product sold or service provided. Whilst it is generally very easy to set up, each transaction fee charged to you by PayPal is significantly higher and some guests simply may not want to pay through the PayPal platform. Stripe is a cost-effective alternative designed for high-volume e-commerce style payments. You have access to a useful dashboard which is fully customisable for your business needs, allowing you to see incoming and outgoing payments centrally within your business. Don't get me wrong, it's a more complex system than PayPal that takes some setting up, however, with the help of customer support, once it's online and operational I see it as a superior platform for our needs. I encourage you to research the various platforms and come up with your own conclusion as to which best fits your business practices. A core benefit to using payment platforms, in general, is the security checks performed on the customer, including identification checks and the monitoring of potentially fraudulent payments. As a new business owner, I imagine this is the last thing on your mind, but these services can support you with your regulatory Anti-Money Laundering duties which to me is worth the small transactional fee. Speaking of fees, payment platforms will charge some form of transactional fee for each payment made. As of the time of writing, Stripe will charge 1.4% of the transaction value + 20p for UK card payments, and 2.9% + 20p for international payments. Other platforms will be fewer, others will be more. In the scheme of the income generated from operating R2RSA properties, it's fractional and not worth skimping on. You can also utilise Stripe to invoice customers for sourcing fees or direct bookings outside of the OTA's, as well as using the platform to support the end-of-year tax calculations.

I've provided an initial flavour into the utility provided by payment gateway platforms here, but I'd again encourage you to look into which will suit your business best and get set up with their services as soon as possible. Do remember, if you don't get on with the selected platform, you're not tied contractually, so you're welcome to shop around the service providers until you find the most optimised for your preferences. It's worth noting that if, like me, you have a trusted management company controlling your properties, then there is no real need to utilise a payment platform. You'll receive a report and payments monthly with your NET income generated, so your company won't experience the high volumes of payments which the management company will.

Direct Bookings vs OTA Bookings

As you have seen in the above sections of this book, bookings for a serviced accommodation property largely come from Online Travel Agencies as these hold a significant market share due to the convenience they provide consumers. Whilst these platforms generate the majority of a host's income, the use of these services comes at a significant cost, averaging around 14% - 19% in commission fees as bookings are achieved through these platforms. Direct bookings on the other hand are different. As the name suggests, a direct booking is where a guest will book to stay within your property by paying your company directly, as opposed to going through an OTA platform. The net result is, on average, a 14% - 19% saving, which you can either pocket yourself, or share with your guest to incentivise them to book directly in the future. For example, say your booking fee's average 15%. If you offered a direct booking client a 7.5% discount, this offers incentivisation to book your apartment in the future. Parallel to this, you're achieving 7.5% more income than you would have through an OTA booking. It's a win-win. I'll let you determine a ratio in which you're happy to share with a guest, if any.

In theory, then, you may wonder why anyone would list on OTA platforms at all. The fact of the matter is that these platforms generate a significant amount of advertising for your property through marketing campaigns and market share. Despite the booking commission, it would most likely be catastrophic for your occupancy rates if you weren't listed on these platforms. Therefore, despite the costs, it's essentially a requirement to be listed on the OTA platforms. However, this doesn't mean that we shouldn't be pushing for direct bookings where possible to increase your occupancy and profit margins further, so we'll look into some techniques around how to achieve this. Let's first look at our target market to understand who we can contact to generate direct bookings. Firstly, we have what I call our *"domestic sales"*, which are made up of retail guests looking for a staycation or holiday. In the opening few years of your business, this category of people will be hard to contact directly as there is no live register giving you the names and contact details of anyone that's looking for a holiday. It would frankly be quite disturbing if there was. The way the OTA platforms directly acquire the attention of this group of people is through marketing, which is an expensive process. Sure, you can pay for some Facebook ads and post your property in free holiday groups, but I don't personally see this as a high ratio of return. Put it this way, what are the odds that you post in a free group, and there so happens to be a person which a) sees the post b) is looking for a break in your specific area and c) decides to book your property through a much smaller, untested platform compared to that of the OTAs. I'm not saying it's impossible, and it's a hell of a lot better than doing nothing, but like I say the ratio of business gained compared to the time put into this lead generation method I believe to be quite poor. This brings us to our second category of people which I call *"commercial sales"*. This category is made up of businesses or people looking for accommodation for business purposes. People in this category include, but are not limited to:

- Construction & Design Contractors, requiring accommodation whilst on a local worksite
- Insurance Company Clients, needing temporary homing after a claim
- Local Business Clients, visiting local branches
- Doctors, visiting local healthcare facilities
- Homeowners, looking for temporary housing during staggered exchange dates.
- Pilots/air hostesses, requiring accommodation between flights

Commercial sales have the potential to be far more predictable, in the sense that you have the power to physically find local businesses through a desktop exercise to target them directly. You can almost always find a local business's contact number, email address or physically attend their office. As the proactive property manager, it's your job to establish a relationship with those businesses to receive direct bookings. If you are targeting companies directly, you'll need to place yourself in their position and ask yourself, *what would make them choose our property over competitors or hotels?* I can't speak for all businesses, but I can almost guarantee cost is going to be the primary factor. You could produce a brochure for your property, demonstrating the cost saving, per room, compared to that of a hotel. Demonstrate the facilities over and above a hotel room (i.e. kitchen, living spaces etc.), and offer discounts as discussed earlier as you're bypassing OTA commission fees. In short, provide as much evidence as to why you're offering a superior service. Once you have any documentation you need, take a tour around the local area and identify building developments, note down the construction company working at the site and contact them. If you're feeling brave, you could walk into the site reception area and pitch to the site manager face-to-face. If you're targeting long-term direct bookings, then I would advise focusing on identifying insurance companies, construction sites and estate agents who can offer clients temporary accommodation between contract exchanges. If you're able to secure clients from these businesses, you may well be looking at bookings measured in months rather than nights, so it's worth the hassle. If you perform well, it's likely these companies will give you repeat direct bookings in the future. To summarise, I believe chasing commercial sales is a more realistic approach to gaining a higher percentage of direct bookings for your efforts. What I can say with certainty is that, by simply putting the time into proactively looking for businesses, you'll be doing a grander job than most other management companies who simply rely on the OTAs. Don't be afraid to be proactive in your approach, rather than reactive, as in the medium to long term this will result in more profitability for your business.

Finding Cleaners & Their Role

This section is only applicable if you're either managing your own units or other companies' units. If you're paying for a management service, they should fulfil all the cleaning requirements for the property without any input from yourself. Good quality cleaners and cleaning companies that support short-term rental businesses by maintaining the properties' condition, operation and tidiness are absolute heroes in my book. Without our cleaners and their keen ability to react to short notice cleaning schedules, none of these services we offer would be possible. Aside from the obvious cleaning services, cleaners are our eyes and ears, providing valuable feedback to property managers regarding property condition, any damages and general replenishments required. Before you start enquiring about cleaning services, you need to lay out exactly what you are expecting from a cleaner. If you're going to contact cleaners directly outside of specialised software, which we'll look into later, you'll need to produce a checklist with some basic activities for the cleaner to attend to. This is common practice, and in some cases sufficient, however, I prefer to be a bit more professional. I would recommend drafting up a simple Service Level Agreement, highlighting the necessary services you're expecting from your selected cleaner. To be clear, you don't need to be a solicitor or a lawyer to draft up a service-level agreement, it's a simple non-contractual agreement that defines the role of a cleaner and your expectations as well as the role of the property manager (your company). There is no need to go overboard here, I would recommend producing an agreement which contains the following sections:

- A cover page, including the cleaning company name with a signature box, the management company name with a signature box and the date of signature.
- An overview description of the agreement, including any agreement goals and objectives
- The duration of the agreement (although not enforceable in this type of agreement)
- A list of services expected from your cleaner, which I'll expand on below.
- A list of your obligations, which I'll expand on below

You need to clearly define exactly what you expect from your cleaner, point by point, and also explain how often you expect these points to be performed. When a cleaner attends your property, you may want them to perform the following cleaning activities:

- Changing the linen and washing old linen
- Washing and putting away the dishes
- Cleaning toilets and bathrooms
- Kitchen cleaning
- Wiping door handles, light switches and cupboard handles and picture frames etc.
- Property hoovering and mopping
- Cleaning around, and moving the furniture, to clean
- Replacing bin liners and taking out the rubbish
- Checking and reporting damages
- Reporting low inventory, such as coffee, bread, milk, toiletries etc.
- Reporting damages to the management company

Defining your expectations for a cleaner within a service level agreement or even a checklist, will help them provide you with an accurate price for their cleaning services. A few things to consider when selecting a cleaner. Do some initial due diligence into the company, looking for positive reviews and confirming they have the correct public liability insurance in place in case of accidental damage or injury. You need to agree with the cleaner as to whether your company will provide the cleaning products or not. Generally, cleaners will have their own cleaning products, so I would personally let them utilise their array of products and contain any cost within their quotation. I'll stress again that you want your cleaner to be fully aware that they are signing up for a cleaning regime that is inconsistent. Your cleaners need to understand that they are responsible for checking the booking calendar through your channel manager to understand when their services are required. The best way to mitigate confusion is to go with a cleaner that already cleans serviced accommodation properties as all of the above will be expected.

In terms of your obligations as a management company, the information you should provide, but is not limited to, includes:

- The property address and parking arrangements
- Property access arrangements (through a lockbox or key nest)
- Payment dates and when you'll pay. Some cleaners may want to invoice per clean, others may want a monthly payment depending on the number of cleans performed
- Provide information about what time the cleaners can operate (i.e. between checkout and check-in times)
- Information about storage of materials, products and inventory

There are a few locations where you can recruit cleaners for your business. As I'm a bit of a stickler for trying to support local businesses, I've found that advertising for cleaners on social media platforms within local Facebook groups harbours a lot of enquiries to take on the work. Simply advertise the property size, add some general cleaning requirements and you should receive a substantial number of cleaners commenting on your post. From here, it's a simple case of sending over your service level agreement and confirming whether they are suitable to perform the work. Alternatively, if you're looking to reduce your workload and streamline your business, you can use yet more software designed to connect cleaners with hosts. If this sounds suitable for you, I've got a couple of options to consider:

- TIDY
- TurnoverBnB

I've personally only used TurnoverBnB, so I can't comment on the quality of service provided by TIDY. Feel free to look into TIDY if you're looking for an alternative. TurnoverBnB is a software which allows you to connect with cleaners by listing your property on the platform and having the cleaning companies come to you in a 'bid for work' format. Your property listing will be seen by cleaners using the platform where you'll receive requests to take on your cleaning requirements. For me, the most useful aspect of this platform is that it's designed for serviced accommodation, therefore, the cleaners on the platform know the process. When using TurnoverBnB, you can produce customisable checklists for the cleaners on the platform, meaning you can do away with a service level agreement or a manual checklist I discussed earlier. Both you and your cleaner can access the software via the mobile app which, at the time of writing, either synchronises with the common OTA's: Booking.com, AirBnb & Vrbo directly or your channel management software. Make sure to check on the TurnoverBnB website that your channel management software is compatible, as of the time of writing, Tokeet is the only integrated platform from my suggestions earlier in the book. The net result is that your cleaners know exactly when to attend your property based on calendar data and are experienced with serviced accommodation requirements. The good news is that your first property on TurnoverBnB is free, therefore there is no harm in engaging with this software on a trial basis.

Property Security

Each management company needs to consider how to provide guests and cleaners with simple and reliable access to the property whilst keeping it secure. I shall suggest a few options for consideration; each requiring different levels of intrusive installation. I would recommend discussing these options with your landlord so that there are no unwelcome surprises on their part when they next visit the property. Your first option, which appears to be the most commonly used, is a lockbox system. A lockbox is a small, often metallic, enclosure which accommodates the property keys. The basic lock boxes have a rotary combination lock, which guests and cleaners will be given the combination to when entering the building. Whilst cost-effective, to me the glaring problem here is that unless someone is changing your combination daily, each past guest will have access to the property by simply remembering the combination. I suppose you could ask your cleaner to change the combination of the lock box when they visit, however, to me it's only a matter of time before something gets lost in translation and a guest gets stuck outside the property. At a greater cost, you could look into a smart lockbox solution. These lock boxes use a keypad, instead of a rotary combination lock, for entering the access code. These systems can be set up in such a way that cleaners can have their own codes and guests will have a separate code which is changed automatically after every stay and is notified to the management company via an app.

Not to mention, these smart locks are a much sturdier solution. Trust me, you are not getting into an advanced lockbox system without heavy machinery, whereas I have heard of cheap lockbox systems being smashed with relative ease. I personally like to instil confidence in the landlord by installing more expensive smart lockbox systems. I like to think that this shows that I truly care about their property and possessions, so the additional cost of a smart lockbox doesn't phase me. The installation of these lock boxes is simple, you will usually be provided with masonry plugs and it's a case of drilling the external surface, entering the plugs and fixing the box to the external facade of the building. If you're setting up in a freehold property, then I would simply speak with the landlord, advise him/her where you're going to install the lock box and check if they are happy for you to proceed. I'd advise against installing the lock boxes on rendering, as you'll likely cause cracks and once removed, the fixing points will be an eyesore. If you have acquired a leasehold property, say within an apartment block, you need to check with the management company if/where you can install lockboxes, even if the landlord gives you the go-ahead. From my experience, the management company will often reject the proposal of installing a lockbox, therefore, you're often forced down the route of the next option. An alternative to lockboxes is a service called KeyNest, a system of locations where you can store your property keys for guests and cleaners to collect. Keynest is an online service which has partnered with local vendors in towns and cities across the United Kingdom who store the keys on the host's behalf. The host deposits the keys upon setting a property up and generates a collection code for the first guest. Subsequently, the guest returns the keys after checkout, a collection code is generated, and the next guest or cleaner collects the keys before the next check-in. There is an introductory video to the Keynest System on their website. A significant benefit to the system is that you can track key locations & check-in/checkout times. You would be surprised how many guests don't return keys to lockboxes, which only becomes apparent once your next guest or cleaner arrives. If the guest checkout time is 11:00 am, with a Keynest, you know that the key should be returned in the next half an hour or so. If it reaches 11:30 am, and your key hasn't been checked in, you can contact the guest and secure the key before its next use. This is simply improving the service for all the subsequent guests ensuring there are no access issues to the property. Before using this service, however, there are a few things to consider. Firstly, you need to search the location of your property on the Keynest website and ensure there is a deposit point ideally within walking distance of your property. Put yourself in the position of the guest; would you appreciate having to walk a mile to pick up your keys? I'll take a location that I know well as an example, Harrogate. As of the time of writing, Harrogate has two Keynest locations, both on the northern side of the town centre. If I was to set an apartment up even in the centre, the closest Keynest location is a 14-minute, 0.7-mile, walk in either direction. As a guest, if you caught the train in for a relaxing weekend away to your central location property, I imagine you'd be pissed if you found out you had to take your luggage on a 1.4-mile round trip. In addition to this, the convenience store the Keynest is located within is only open 10:00 am - 21:00 pm (Monday to Saturday) and 11:00 am - 19:00 pm (Sunday). This will put access restriction times on your property, which may cause contractors to steer towards competitors as they often need access to the property at all times throughout the night. To conclude then, if you're to use this service, don't assume that there is a suitable pickup nearby. Try to find a local service within a couple of minutes that's preferably a 24-hour location. These sites are much more common in built-up cities. You may struggle in smaller, less populated areas. The Keynest service is a paid one, offering a pay-as-you-go service of £5.95 ex VAT per key collection, a monthly plan of

£21.95 ex VAT per property and a yearly plan at £16.96 ex VAT per property, billed annually. These can be found on the pricing page of the Keynest website. Make sure that you consider any ongoing costs of the Keynest subscription in your financial calculations if you're to use this service.

Now we've reviewed the access security of the property, let's look at what we can do to secure the property once guests have accessed it. A common objection landlords and letting agents will raise is the subject of parties, breakages and damage. The problem for hosts is that you don't know which guests are going to be a dream and which are going to be a menace, aside from those guests who have good reviews on the OTAs. New guests without a review rating are a complete unknown. To combat this, I want to discuss a product known as a Minut device. This is a single sensory system which alerts a management company to various conditions within the property. The device offers the following features:

- Noise Level Monitoring
- Crowd Detection
- Temperature Monitoring
- Humidity Monitoring
- Security Alarm interface
- Movement Monitoring (when the property is unoccupied)
- Window/Glass breakage detection

Management companies can utilise both noise level monitoring and crowd detection to detect if the property is being used for unauthorised parties/gatherings. Note that the device does not record sound, it simply monitors decibels, so the privacy of guests is not breached with this installation. The other services the device monitors are a bonus, it's up to you whether you want to integrate the system with the building alarm; I personally do not to avoid accidental alarm activation as there are many different stakeholders which enter and leave the premises. The application of the device is simple. Firstly, identify which room is likely to be used in the event of a party. In most cases, it's either the hallway or the living room. The device is provided with a backplate, layered with adhesive. Simply stick the backplate on the ceiling (they do also provide a screw which I would recommend using) and clip the remainder of the device to the backplate. You will need to charge the battery occasionally, which you can add to your cleaners' to-do list bi-weekly. Simply connect to the mobile app, and you're in operation. The Minut device comes in different price packages. As of the time of writing you have two subscription models to choose from. You can either opt for a £50 upfront sensor cost and a £120/year subscription in the "Standard" plan which offers the services listed above. Alternatively, you can choose the "Pro" Plan costing £180/year, with a free sensor and offers additional advantages such as channel manager integration. You can find out more about the product on the Minut website.

The above discussion points are definitely significant and I recommend they are at least considered during the set-up period of your property. However, if you have a management company managing your property, it's unlikely they will discuss the above points with you, especially the Minut device. If this is something you wish to implement within your property, discuss it with your management company, where you'll most likely have to purchase and install it yourself.

Arranging the Property Services

Even if your properties are managed on your behalf, all of the following expenditures and bills will need to be in the company director/company's name. Therefore, it will be your responsibility to set up your apartment services whether you are the property manager or not. If applicable, have a discussion with your management company about which services you're looking to proceed with and make sure they agree with your choices, not that they won't, but communication is always recommended. As I have discussed earlier in this book, there are typical home services that you will need to arrange for the property. To summarise again, these include:

- Council tax
- Electricity & gas
- Water
- Broadband
- TV licence

From the financial calculations performed in previous chapters, you should have a general idea of the cost associated with each of these services, but now you simply need to apply for each service with the respective service provider.

Council Tax

To set up council tax within your property, it's a case of simply contacting your local council and following their registration procedure. Each council is different, so I cannot take you through the specific procedure, but a simple review of your local councils' website will take you to some form of registration page. Simply enter the property postcode into the government website, add the specific address, and it will provide the applicable local authority and council tax bracket. Council tax rules change, so the following text is true as of the time of writing, however, always check with your local authority to ensure you are paying for the correct type of council tax applicable to your property and its use.

By simply registering your R2RSA property with the local council, you may well end up paying the standard domestic council tax charge applicable for that property size, value and location. When we first did this exercise in the financial breakdown, it was for the worst-case scenario outcome and therefore conservative. However, if your property meets certain criteria, it will be considered a "Furnished Holiday Let" and therefore will be categorised within the "Holiday Let Business Rate" tax bracket. Note that in the following paragraphs I'm using the term "holiday let" and "R2RSA property" interchangeably here as a holiday let relates to the government website of which this information is derived from. To fall into this category, the following criteria need to apply to your property:

- The property needs to be fully furnished
- Your property must be available to let on a short-term basis for at least 210 days per year
- If your furnished holiday let is rented out by the same guest for more than 31 days, there shouldn't be more than 155 days of this type of 'long term' occupation per year
- Your property must be rented out as holiday accommodation to the public for at least 105 days of the 210 days you have made it available

If your property has a rateable value (estimated annual rental value) of less than £12,000 per year, then you will fall under small business rate relief and not pay any business rates. For properties with a rateable value of £12,001 to £15,000, the rate of relief will go down gradually from 100% to 0%. So, for your first property under a specific council's legislation, you will most likely have either significant or total council tax relief. There are a few things to consider here. Firstly, the process for these applications and exemptions can be a lengthy one, several months at least. In most cases then, you will start off operating your property under standard domestic council tax rates until this process is concluded. That's not a problem though, as we used these higher figures to calculate our profitability in the financial calculations section. Secondly, I'll stress again, tax rules change. Therefore, I don't recommend removing council tax from your calculations. As you start to scale your portfolio in a single location, the applicable tax rates and reliefs begin to become more complicated, and I think outside of the scope of this introductory book. The specific local council will be able to advise on the process you'll need to follow should you become more aggressive in your property acquisition.

Energy (Electricity & Gas)

At the time of writing, we are operating R2RSA properties in a period where war intensifies in Ukraine, causing a nationwide energy crisis and thus soaring energy prices as a result. More than ever then it's important to try to minimise your energy bill by getting the best possible energy price. Unfortunately, there is no secret, at least that I'm aware of, that can provide hosts with cost-effective energy prices compared to domestic properties. Therefore, it's a review of the comparison websites to find the best price possible. A couple of suggestions include:

- Uswitch
- Money Supermarket

I do have a couple of suggestions for you to help combat the soaring energy prices. You could invest in a smart thermostat, subject to the landlord's permission, which will allow you to restrict excessive energy use via temperature control within the property. If you are to implement this type of restriction, I would recommend not going too far as you don't want guests complaining about the property feeling cold. I'm suggesting potentially limiting the temperature range from 16°C - 24°C. It's also advisable to request that your cleaner checks the heating hasn't been left on nor the windows left open at the property. Adding a polite request within your guest introduction pack to turn the heating, lights and other appliances off once a guest leaves is reasonable. You will find that as long as it isn't a hassle, guests will generally help out where they can. If you haven't experienced an energy provider transfer before, I want to reassure you that during this period, your property won't go without electricity and gas. Apply for a new provider as soon as possible as the existing provider will most likely keep you on the existing property tariff, or put you on a standard energy tariff, which is usually quite expensive. Once you have found a new provider, they will typically accommodate the transfer from the old provider. The landlord should be able to advise who the old provider is. There is very little to be done on your part aside from applying for a new provider. Alternatively, if the existing provider happens to be offering the best price, have discussions with their representatives to understand the tariff end date and whether you can continue it at the existing price. Although I've not personally experienced one, if you're setting up within an apartment complex, you may well have to use a pre-pay metre which reduces as energy is consumed within the property. In these instances, you will top up the credit on the pre-pay meter as and when your credit is reduced due to energy consumption. You still have the right to switch suppliers, however, your landlord may have a clause within your company let contract suggesting a "preferred supplier". You may still switch suppliers; however, you may have to return to the preferred supplier when your tenancy closes. Your landlord, building management or letting agent should be able to advise how much flexibility you have on a case-by-case basis if you're working with a prepaid metre. You simply need to ask the question.

Water

Arranging a water supply is simple as there is usually a single supplier per geographical area. Simply enter the property location within the water supplier website, linked in the end of book resources, and you'll quickly find out which company supplies water to that area. Most water suppliers will have some form of access page which asks a series of questions about the property size and occupancy. The result of your answers will advise a general estimated monthly cost. If you consume more or less water than the estimate suggested, your water supplier will automatically adjust your monthly payments. Simply register, and the water supplier will start charging you for water use. There will again be no loss of water during the property acquisition stage assuming you take fairly swift action registering with the provider.

Broadband

As touched on earlier in the book, broadband is the only service which may cause delay during the acquisition stage. In the past, I have experienced up to a 2 - 3 week delay due to the broadband suppliers stated install date. You want to apply for your internet services as soon as you secure the property. In the interim, a pre-paid 4G dongle can be installed within the property for a couple of weeks. Once again, comparison websites are recommended to secure the best broadband prices. I suggest either:

- Comparethemarket
- Money Supermarket

I won't go into much more detail as the application process is very simple. I will advise, if you're entering a fixed contract, try to secure a 1-year fix as this will most likely align with your company let break clause. Otherwise, say you applied for a 2-year fix, in the event the landlord wants to activate the break clause 12 months in, you may be liable for an early termination charge on your fixed contract with the broadband supplier. You will already be out of pocket because of the eviction, so additional cancellation fees won't be welcome.

TV Licence

To attain a TV licence, simply apply for a new property licence at the TV licencing website. This will allow all of your guests to enjoy television services as well as catch-up services such as All 4, ITV and BBC iplayer. You can either pay monthly or yearly for your subscription, I'll leave that decision to you, but there isn't a significant price difference between the two.

Emergencies and Repairs

As with any property investment, you're inevitably going to have to rectify some form of emergency. Whether it's caused by a guest, or simply some hardware becoming faulty, it is most likely going to happen, so we need to be prepared. It's worth noting that in most company let contracts, it's made clear that the company, or tenant, will be responsible for general property repairs. Exclusions to this include structural repairs, repairs to incoming services and repairs to the heating system. You need to understand which repairs you are financially responsible for at the start of your tenancy, which will be laid out in the company let contract. If a repair at the property is required, whether it's your financial responsibility or not, you'll need to rectify the issue as quickly as possible. If the repair falls on the landlord's shoulders, you need to let them know as soon as possible. During this conversation, you can offer to arrange the remedial works on their behalf to speed the process up. If you are going to follow this approach, send the landlord any quotation you receive for the work and request payment from them. A common example is the boiler breaking down. I would recommend gathering two or three quotes from different businesses, forwarding them to the landlord for review. You could even pay yourself, but if you do, you at least have to ensure the landlord is happy with the cost and is obliged to refund you for the costs associated with the work contractually. If not, leave it in the landlord's hands as you may not be able to claim the costs back. Alternatively, the cooker, TV, Microwave or some other appliance may become faulty. As discussed earlier, the cleaner will make you aware of this during their inspection, or the guest may contact you directly if the breakage occurs during their stay. If you are handy and local, you can of course rectify the issue yourself. If not, there are emergency call-out services which you can leverage. The first group of companies I will mention are property repair services. These companies/services offer core repair works on the property such as plumbing, drainage, central heating, electrics etc. They are a 24-hour service and have a nationwide network of trades staff to perform emergency repairs. Alternatively, if the damages that need repairing are less critical to the property's operation, like an appliance replacement for example, then you simply need to take to google and search for local 24-hour handymen. MyBuilder allows you to describe what work you need performing and post it to its network of tradesmen. Both of the above options won't be cheap; however, they will be quick rectification services to get your property back to 100% operation. Fingers crossed, you won't need to use these services often, if at all, but at least you now have the information if you do.

Virtual Assistants

Whether you're building your R2RSA portfolio or scaling your client managing services, you will reach a point where your ability to proactively manage the portfolio as well as respond to every guest query, request and complaint becomes almost impossible. The fear of profit loss, or having to hire someone within your business, may drive you to stretch yourself to a point which is detrimental to the business's growth and quality of service. At this point, I want to touch on virtual assistants. Known as VAs, a virtual assistant is an independent contractor that offers remote administrative support for your business based on your specific requirements. Finding an experienced VA specialising in our industry is a sure way to free up your time to focus on bringing on more management clients and finding direct bookings as I discussed earlier. One of the most prominent perks of hiring an experienced VA is their skill. I am happy to admit that an experienced VA will often, dare I say, outperform me due to their experience in managing AirBnB properties, and it frees my time to work on other projects, so it's a win-win in terms of business performance. Their ability to produce great listings will make your properties more attractive to guests, subsequently, their excellent communication skills will keep those guests happy for the duration of their stay. VAs require no office space, nor do they require hardware, as they'll work remotely from their chosen location. When I refer to hiring "a virtual assistant", as in singular, this is inaccurate. When working with VAs, you're often working with a business containing operatives on 24-hour cycles able to respond to problems 24/7. Before contacting a VA, it would be wise to create a list of activities you would like to pass over so that they can accurately price their work as well as understand your expectations. If you wish, and it's the route I would personally take, you could draft yet another Service Level Agreement similar to what I discussed earlier in the chapter for cleaner acquisition. Clearly define your expectations, and then you can issue it to various VA companies and see which will fit your requirements best. So, what can a VA do for you and your business? Below are a few suggestions:

- Respond to guest questions, queries and complaints between bookings
- Issue information to guests upon booking, such as a welcome pack, parking instructions, check-in methods, house rules etc
- Schedule cleaners and maintainers for the property
- Launch properties and write descriptions on the OTA's via your channel management service
- Accounting and bookkeeping
- Manage your company's social media accounts
- Produce monthly management reports to investors through your channel management service

It may take a few interviews to find the right VA for your business, but finding the correct one can relieve you of a significant amount of work. Not every VA will be competent to perform all the tasks listed above, and it would be unwise to hand everything over without some form of review/assurance process from yourself as the company director, especially tasks associated with investor payment reports. However, the basic items listed above (guest management & property listings) will be second nature to most short-term let VA support companies thus providing you with a viable opportunity to outsource. To find a VA for your company, simply take to the freelancing websites below and post your project requirements giving as much detail as possible about what works, out of the list above, you expect their business to take on. This will give you the best opportunity of having credible, competent VAs bidding for your work. Through these websites, you'll be able to communicate with VA companies where you can ask for previous work examples, current projects and arrange an interview date.

- Freelancer
- Fiver

Different VA companies have different pricing structures, so I can't accurately advise at what cost you can acquire VA services, however, you will often be paying VAs for an hourly rate service. Some VAs may work with you on a rolling contract, whereas others will offer various pricing plans to lock in a specific number of hours with their company, which often results in being the most cost-effective option.

You may well be wondering, what is the difference between a trained virtual assistant and a R2RSA management company? They certainly do appear to be responsible for similar tasks. In theory, a competent VA could perform almost all management tasks, so why hire a management company? If I was to respond to this question, I would suggest a virtual assistant company is a great tool to reduce management workload, allowing you as a management company director to spend time acquiring more clients and greater bookings (increasing occupancy) for your existing clients. This is where I believe the distinction between a VA and a management company is. A virtual assistant won't have the same invested interest in the success of a property as the property owner or their management company, as we're paid via the property's profits or a percentage-based commission. We are the ones that require maximum profitability and therefore are motivated to proactively explore direct bookings and new properties for the portfolio. With a fixed hourly rate, I don't believe a VA has the same motivation. Not to say they won't do great work, I've already admitted that they will be significantly better and more efficient than I would be at some tasks, I just believe they're better suited to being used as a support pillar for passing over simple, yet time-consuming, work within your management business.

The Management Process Summary

Now that we have looked at the various tools utilised by management companies to enhance efficiency, I will describe the basic process used by management companies when onboarding properties into their portfolio. This list is not comprehensive enough to cover all aspects of management and may even be somewhat insulting to those expert management companies that have a wealth of knowledge about management outside of my recommendations. However, it will at least provide you with a reasonable structure for building your management services, if you so wish. I will assume that by this point, you have your strategy defined (Chapter 3) and your business set up and compliant (Chapter 5).

Managing your own portfolio, for the purposes of Income Method 1, Chapter 3

1) Ensure you have a payment platform, such as Stripe, integrated with your business bank account to accept payments through the OTA booking platforms.
2) Secure, set up and stage the property to a high quality through the implementation of high-quality furnishings. Use the example furniture list within the end of book resources to ensure you have the necessary furniture for serviced accommodation use.
3) Ensure all the property services, such as electricity, water, broadband and council tax are registered and connected.
4) Arrange for a professional photographer with experience in property staging to take professional photos of the property ready for listing.
5) Whether you are utilising a lockbox or Keynest system, ensure the access strategy to your property is operational. Install any additional security features, such as Minut devices, within the property ready for listing.
6) Advertise the cleaning requirements through local sources, TIDY or Turnoverbnb to secure cleaning services for the property. Provide the cleaners with a detailed list of activities to perform, through a checklist or service level agreement, providing them with access to your properties calendar and access arrangements.
7) Conclude the nightly rates to be applied to your listing either through manual input, based on a desktop analysis, or through the use of dynamic pricing software such as Pricelabs or Wheelhouse. If applying nightly rates manually, ensure you consider weekends, holidays, and events within your nightly rate determination.
8) Utilise your channel management software in conjunction with the OTA's to list your properties, allowing guests to start booking. Produce a well written listing including relevant guest information. Good example listing information can be

found on Airbnb from host listings with "Superhost" status. Alternatively, utilise experienced virtual assistants to offload this activity for all future listings.

9) Once the property is live, provide responsive support to guests during the booking and accommodation process. Answer queries in a timely manner to boost your chances of receiving strong reviews. Alternatively, utilise experienced virtual assistants to offload this activity for all future listings.

10) Identify local businesses under the branch of "commercial sales" described earlier in this chapter. Produce any documentation required which proves the benefits of your accommodation over local competitors. Contact these businesses and pitch your accommodation, with the goal of receiving direct bookings over bookings through the OTA platforms.

11) Make monthly rental payments to the landlord through your businesses bank account manually or through a direct debit. Respond to landlord queries throughout the tenancy and ensure you attend to any damages/repairs that occur due to guest usage.

Managing properties for other investors, for the purposes of Income Method 2, Chapter 3

1) Obtain any documentation you require for the management of R2RSA properties. This includes a management contract plus the various software packages discussed earlier in this chapter.

2) Ensure you have a payment platform, such as Stripe, integrated with your business bank account to accept payments through the OTA booking platforms.

3) Determine your management fee (%) and determine the factor of which that fee is applied. For example, a common structure is a 15% fee on gross property income, excluding

property bills. Typical management fees are between 15% - 20%.

4) Find investors using the Facebook groups described earlier in this book. Make contact with these investors via messenger, offering your management services whether they are acquiring properties through another sourcer or through your own sourcing services, should you offer this.

5) Arrange a face-to-face meeting, or Zoom call, with investors to discuss details about their upcoming R2RSA properties of which they need management support. You need to understand the property's location, size, amenities, contract duration etc. Discuss your services, pricing structure and present examples of past successes, if possible. If this will be the first property you have managed, you may come across resistance due to your inexperience. You can either look at a reduced management rate or alternatively build experience managing your own R2RSA portfolio first.

6) Based on the property presented by the investor, I would recommend performing your own financial analysis to confirm that the investors property will be profitable. If the investment looks poor, highlight this to the investor and discuss whether they still wish to proceed. If you manage a property that performs financially poorly, it will most likely end up being a waste of your time and may lead to bad management reviews. Confirm that the investor's property is going to be/has been secured using a company let agreement.

7) Should the investor wish to proceed with your services, issue your management contract to the investor, populated with the relevant property information and contractual content discussed earlier in this chapter.

8) Confirm with the investor who is going to set up the property. You can offer to charge your client an additional fee to set up

the property on their behalf. A typical set up fee ranges from £300 - £500, which typically includes photography, furniture building, inventory checks, lockbox/Keynest installation and the property listing. You can invoice your client prior to starting the work. If the investor wishes to set up their own property, recommend that they take professional photographs and use high quality furnishings, as this will enhance their bookings and reviews. Use the example furniture list within the end of book resources as a guide to check that the necessary furniture for serviced accommodation is in place.

9) Ensure that the investor has set up the property services, such as electricity, water, broadband and council tax.

10) Whether the property utilises a lockbox or Keynest system, ensure the access strategy to the investors property is operational. Discuss with the investor whether they wish to install additional security features, such as Minut devices, within the property.

11) Advertise the cleaning requirements through local sources, TIDY or Turnoverbnb to secure cleaning services for the property. Provide the cleaners with a detailed list of activities to perform, through a checklist or service level agreement, providing them with access to your properties calendar and access arrangements.

12) Conclude the nightly rates to be applied to the listing either through manual input, based on a desktop analysis, or through the use of dynamic pricing software such as Pricelabs or Wheelhouse. If applying nightly rates manually, ensure you consider weekends, holidays, and events within your nightly rate determination.

13) List the property on your channel management software in conjunction with the OTA's to list your properties, allowing guests to start booking. Produce a well written listing

including relevant guest information. Good example listing information can be found on Airbnb from host listings with "Superhost" status. Alternatively, utilise experienced virtual assistants to offload this activity for all future listings.

14) Once the property is live, provide responsive support to guests during the booking and accommodation process. Answer queries in a timely manner to boost your chances of receiving strong reviews. Alternatively, utilise experienced virtual assistants to offload this activity for all future listings.

15) Identify local businesses under the branch of "commercial sales" described earlier in this chapter. Produce any documentation required which proves the benefits of your investor's accommodation over local competitors. Contact these businesses and pitch the accommodation, with the goal of receiving direct bookings over bookings through the OTA platforms.

16) If you have agreed that the investor will pay the landlord the rental figure directly, ensure that rent has been paid by the investor monthly. If you have agreed that you, the management company, will pay the rent on behalf of the investor, issue the investor an invoice for the rental figure, forwarding it to the landlord upon receipt.

17) On a monthly basis, provide profit/loss statements to your investor using the report tool within your channel management software. This will state the total monthly turnover of the property, then subtract OTA commissions, your management fee, cleaning fee's, replenishment fee's, channel management fee's etc., leaving a quantity of capital owed to the investor. Issue this profit/loss statement along with the funds to the investor.

18) Should any damages/repairs be required at the property, inform the investor immediately and await a decision as to how the problem will be rectified.

Should you be operating under Scenario 2 (Limited Time with Disposable Capital, Chapter 3) you may well be looking for management companies to manage your portfolio on your behalf. In this case, the above step by step processes are not applicable. In your position, you need to find a reliable management company with good reviews, excellent performance and experience in R2RSA management. Feel free to contact me should you want management company recommendations.

I want to review how lucrative management, income Method 2 Chapter 3, can be for yourself and your business should you utilise this method as your primary income stream. Management income in particular is impossible to predict as there are various factors of which influence the income produced by each property. Your management contract terms and performance as a manager will directly influence your income, as well as the properties desirability, location and amenities. Therefore, all I can do for the purposes of this calculation, is continue with our previous calculation and suggest that over the next six to twelve months you can reasonably target to acquire five management clients through the methodology described earlier in this chapter. From the example earlier in this chapter, we described that the management fees earned by the management company that particular month, for that particular example property, were £271.20pcm. Assuming identical results from your management portfolio of 5 properties, you can expect to earn an additional £1356.00pcm, or £16,272 annually, in risk free management revenue from your clients. After accounting for 25% corporation tax, this reduces to £1017pcm, or £12,204 annually. We understand that these arbitrary numbers are for example purposes only, but you can see how the acquisition of management clients can contribute to your income in a way that does not require any upfront capital from yourself or your business. Similar to Method 1, your real monthly returns will follow a more sinusoidal relationship as the property performs better or worse throughout the seasons.

Chapter 8 – The Future of R2RSA

As I have presented the reality of R2RSA throughout this book, I hope I have been able to at least inspire you to develop an R2RSA strategy, acquire quality properties legally and provide an overview of how you can use various tools to manage those properties effectively. I believe that the information I have provided up to this point is correct as of the time of writing, but I do also believe the future holds changes for the short-term letting industry. Whilst the content of this chapter is going to include some level of speculation on my part, I thought it would be useful to share my opinions on the future of short-term lettings, backed by present day facts. My predictions for the future are founded on a series of existing and potentially upcoming regulation combined with my understanding of how those in the market currently operate. Any regulations I'm subsequently going to discuss don't affect just those within the Rent to Rent industry, but will affect all listings on the OTA's, including property owners utilising holiday let mortgages and owners simply listing their second homes on the OTA platforms. The purpose of this chapter is to give my view on what I believe the future holds for R2RSA, however, the same restrictions will spill over into other property-related strategies. With this in mind, I believe it's important to also look at the holiday let market as, although it's a different strategy, it's closely related to the R2RSA business model. Before we look into the future, I want to briefly recap the current status of the short-term letting market. As of the time of writing, you can set up an R2RSA property almost anywhere in the UK without restriction. Restrictions and regulations have primarily been applied to London, Scotland and Whales, which we will discuss in later paragraphs. In general, companies are setting properties up for short-term accommodation nationwide outside of these restricted locations. Since mid-2021, post Covid restrictions, the short-term let market has been booming. Companies and individuals are generating healthy cash flow from short-term accommodation properties. For this reason, we continue to see aggressive property acquisition throughout the UK for short term accommodation purposes, both from holiday let investors and R2RSA investors. We are seeing a trend where more and more operators are setting up existing properties for short-term letting purposes, and little has been done in recent years to combat this, as we'll explore. Areas that remain unregulated, providing consistent job opportunities for contractors and attractive amenities for holidayers, will continue to generate serviced accommodation operators' healthy returns. Therefore, it's hard to imagine that the acquisition process will slow without intervention. I'm also going to briefly explain quite a critical difference between those who own property for short-term accommodation purposes, referred to as Holiday Let's, and those who rent properties from landlords using the R2RSA strategy. Individuals, or companies, that own Holiday let properties either own the properties outright, and have very little risk, or have their properties leveraged using mortgage products. Generally speaking, this group of people have to generate less profit with their holiday let properties to break even. Paying an interest-only mortgage monthly will generally equate to less cost than paying a monthly rental figure, as a R2RSA operator has to do, to a landlord. A R2RSA operator is paying off the property owners mortgage, plus an additional profit margin, hence equating to a higher monthly cost. It's worth noting that a holiday let owner has the flexibility to change the property from a holiday let to a residential let, should market conditions become unfavourable. I would like to stress that a R2RSA operator does not have this flexibility as they don't own the property. If market conditions become unfavourable, their rent is still due whether the property is producing positive cash flow or not. Currently the market is booming, but whilst you read the rest of this chapter, I want you to bear in mind the following statement. Subject to market conditions becoming substantially unfavourable for short-term accommodation, for any reason, R2RSA operators are at the most risk of being over-leveraged and unable to meet payment obligations. With that out the way, let's look at the current restrictions in place and see if we can identify a trend in the market direction.

I'll start with the London "90-Day Rule" which is commonly understood as a core short-term let restriction to those in the industry. Looking at data produced by the unit for Evaluation & Policy Analysis at Edge Hill University, in the paper *"Home or hotel? A contemporary challenge in the use of housing stock"*, some simply alarming statistics can be found. Found in the London-based statistics, the paper states that in 2014, 13,327 AirBnB listings were available to the public. By 2017, this number had risen to 55,563 listings, representing a 317% increase. Whilst London has always had restrictions associated with short-term lets and accommodation, it's clear with this rate of listing increase that the laws were hazy at best. As the home-sharing industry by 2015 was growing exponentially, the Deregulation Act 2015 was introduced which provided clarity and relaxation of existing laws around planning permission requirements for short-term accommodation within Greater London. These regulations allowed homeowners to let their property out for up to 90 nights per year without the need to apply for planning permission, which would bring your property under the 'temporary sleeping accommodation' category rather than standard residential property. Interestingly, despite the introduction of the law, the years 2016 and 2017 saw the fastest rate of annual listing growth of 77% & 70% respectively. In 2017, AirBnB themselves physically restricted property listings in Greater London to 90-days. This may well have been the wake-up call for those pursuing short-term rentals in London as the subsequent growth rate from 2018 to 2019 was far more modest at 27% and 13% respectively. If you wish to let a property out for short-term accommodation for longer than 90 days, it must be registered with the local council through a planning permission application form. This will allow you to file for an exemption with the OTA's, allowing your listing to be unrestricted. It's worth noting that homeowners letting a portion of their house out, of which they live, have a 90-day rule exemption as well. It was thought that the increase in short-term accommodation was threatening the housing supply market for both home buyers and renters residing within Greater London, so the local council made it a priority to put measures in place to both clarify the law and reduce the increase of listings in the city, or at least that's the outcome whether or not it was their intention. So why am I telling you this? Within the United Kingdom at least, the London 90-Day rule is the most widely known restriction for short-term accommodation, however, short term let restrictions are not isolated to London.

In more recent times, Scotland has tended towards a similar fate. The Civic Government (Scotland) Act 1982 (Licencing of Short-term Lets) Order 2022 was passed by the Scottish Parliament in January 2022. According to a Scottish Government study on the impact of short-term lets on the local community, in 2016 approximately 10,500 short-term accommodation properties were listed in the country. By 2019, this number had increased to approximately 32,000 listings, representing a 205% increase in 3 years. 50.5% of these listings were concentrated in the City of Edinburgh and the Highlands. From 1st October 2022, new hosts operating in the City of Edinburgh must obtain a licence from their local authority before short-term let operation. The City of Edinburgh falls within what Scotland defined as "a Short Term Let Control Area", meaning a licence is mandatory. Local authorities in other Scottish towns/cities will be able to apply, increasing the geographical boundaries of the control areas in the country. Existing hosts have until 1st April 2023 to acquire a licence. Useful information about the licencing procedure can be found on the Scottish government website, providing more depth around the licence acquisition procedure and exemptions. The passing of the new regulation was consulted with 5600 respondents, of which a staggering 88% agreed with the proposals as it was concluded that short-term lets appeared to exacerbate housing shortages and fuelled a rise in antisocial behaviour.

In France, we are seeing similar restrictions. Brought into force to help ease the pressure on France's *"housing crisis",* The French Court of Cassation ruled in favour of increased short-term let regulation in 2020. The result is that short-term property operators must make a declaration to the town hall to obtain a registration number which must be visible in the property listing, similar to the procedure followed in London. According to information presented by Roche & Cie, letting out your primary residence, or areas of your primary residence is restricted to 120 days per year. Second homes can be rented without a yearly restriction subject to town hall approval. No single tenant can stay in any short-term accommodation for longer than 90-days. In 2020, two landlords renting studio apartments in Paris were subject to a €15,000 fine due to a lack of authorisation from the town hall and the City of Paris.

Aside from city centre locations, UK-based rural areas are also experiencing problems of their own concerning the increase in short-term holiday let demand. The supply of short-term accommodation properties has formed due to what I identify as a *perfect storm* scenario that has been brewing in recent years. Firstly, we had COVID, a global pandemic which generally shut down the international travel sector or at the very least made travelling internationally a riskier, far more painful process for British holidaymakers and businesses. Flights were cancelled, restrictions were put in place, specific countries were red-listed and the isolation period once returning to the UK was highly impractical. The net result, a larger percentage of the British public resorted to "stay-cations" rather than holidaying abroad, immediately increasing demand for holiday locations within the UK border confines. The Office for National Statistics reported that in 2021, 20% fewer people made visits abroad than in 2020, and incredibly 2020 saw a 74.4% decrease from 2019. The shocking decline is as impressive when demonstrated graphically below. To be clear, I'm not suggesting that all of these UK residents suddenly took to holidaying within the border confines, however, it is reasonable to conclude that this data at least contributed to the increased booking demand of UK based short term accommodation.

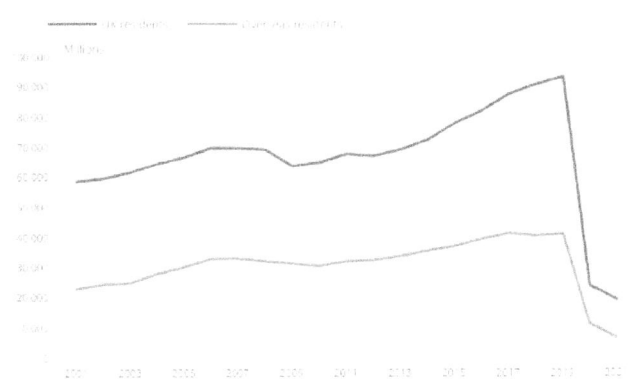

Figure 3: Visits to and from the UK from 2001 to 2021

Figure 4 – Office for National Statistics of Abroad Travel

Although the restrictions of COVID now seem a distant memory in the UK, 2022 research suggests short-term bookings are up 30% on 2021, potentially driven by the current disruption and delays experienced at airports nationally. Taking Cornwall as an example, between 2015 & 2021, a 1000% increase in the number of homes listed for short-term accommodation has been reported, according to the Campaign to Protect Rural England (CPRE). In total, Cornwall reports 25,000 properties as either second homes or holiday lets, which makes up 8% of the total housing stock. This has only been made worse in recent years as international travel demand within the domestic environment has reduced. As I'm writing this section, I'm virtually staring at graffiti sprayed on an unlucky victim's garden wall in Cornwall itself. According to an online publication by The Guardian, the graffiti was produced by second home campaigners. To quote the text sprayed on the wall, *"second homeowners give something back: rent or sell your empty houses to local people at a fair price".* Granted, campaigners are particularly passionate, but the message is clear that the increase in holiday lets/second homes is having an impact on local communities. In June 2022 councillors in Brighton voted in favour of drawing up plans to restrict the ownership of second homes and short term lets. This is reported to be due to COVID spikes in property acquisition, where it's estimated that 3000 properties could be reserved purely for the short term let market through the Online Travel Agency platforms. These statistics are being correlated to a selection of problems by researchers in both rural and heavily populated areas. It's suggested that the increasing short-term accommodation market is pushing house prices up and simultaneously reducing market stock, making housing even more unaffordable for local residents. Long-term renters are being forced out of the market as well, as landlords are looking to increase their profitability by removing tenants from their properties and offering them to the public as short-term accommodation. In addition, local services are suffering, where it's reported that emergency services especially are becoming more and more understaffed to accommodate the increase in the visiting population.

I mentioned a phrase earlier of which I described as the *perfect storm*. Let me explain what I mean by this with the goal of identifying a trend in the market direction. From the above statistics, we've seen that the supply of short-term accommodation in the UK has been increasing. The question is - why? I would hypothesise that short-term accommodation can generate greater profits than long-term lets. Assuming you can achieve reasonable occupancy rates, it's common for a short-term accommodation property to produce greater cash flow than a long-term let. This is due to the high nightly rates charged to guests, as we saw earlier in the financial analysis section, but also is generally a more time-consuming strategy to manage which, as we saw from the time/profitability trade off in Chapter One, typically harbours greater returns. In addition to this, I believe another major factor at play here is the tax relief that a holiday-let property owner receives over a buy-to-let property owner. In 2015, the introduction of the Finance Act 2015 Section 24 meant that buy-to-let landlords could no longer deduct mortgage interest rates from profits generated by a property at year-end, substantially increasing their tax bill. Generally speaking, this meant that a typical buy-to-let landlord earned less year on year for the same property, assuming rental figures remained constant. With this knowledge, hazard a guess as to which property type was excluded from Section 24 - that's right, holiday lets. This meant that almost overnight holiday lets, which in some cases were already more lucrative, became even more lucrative compared to the buy-to-let strategy for an investor able to efficiently operate holiday lets through strong occupancy and efficient management. Not only this, but since holiday lets need to be furnished and presented to a luxury standard, capital allowances for furniture purchases, various renovation activities and fixtures all can be deducted from the end-of-year tax bill. Note that this doesn't only increase profits for the short-term accommodation business, but renovations increase the market value of the property, meaning higher sale values can be achieved when the owner comes to sell. In its most basic sense then, the figure below demonstrates the perfect storm I spoke of earlier, which is made up of two primary factors.

a) The profitability, through tax advantages, for owning a holiday let property using holiday let financing products, compared to owning a buy-to-let property using but-to-let financing products, is currently at a high.

b) The demand for holiday lets has increased due to the growth of OTA platforms such as AirBnB and the restrictions on international travel implied by COVID.

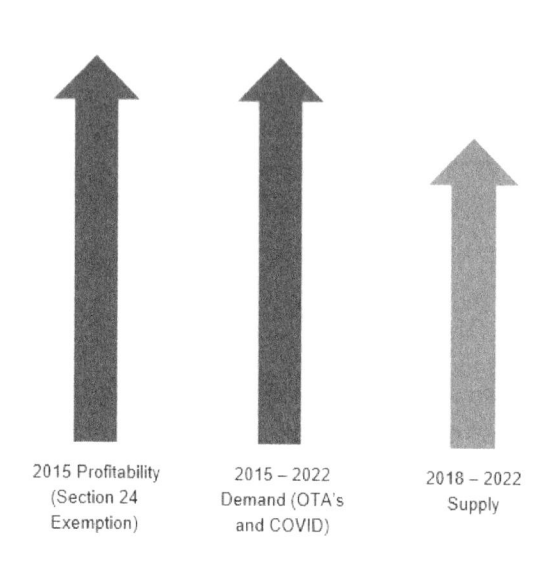

2015 Profitability (Section 24 Exemption) | 2015 – 2022 Demand (OTA's and COVID) | 2018 – 2022 Supply

Figure 5 – The Perfect Storm (Supply & Demand)

The combination of A & B is causing supply to increase to meet the demand, in the medium of an increasing amount of short-term accommodation properties, as individuals want to take advantage of the high demand and profitability. This comes in the form of more Holiday Let operators as well as more R2RSA operators simultaneously. As the market is still booming, I suspect supply hasn't yet met demand, but as we saw from the earlier statistics, the supply is continuing to grow. So, we have profitability at a high, we have demand at a high and we can see the net output of these facts is causing the supply to increase. However, we have seen data that suggests that the problems implied in local economies, services and locals are driven by the increasing supply of short-term accommodation in local economies. The million-pound question for me then is as follows:

Is the increase in supply causing sufficiently severe problems to cause governments to intervene and restrict supply?

Although I am asking this question, it's almost rhetorical, because the unarguable answer to it is yes! How do I know? We have seen already at the start of this chapter that local authorities are applying planning restrictions on short-term accommodation at present day. I've revisited this chapter, thanks to the Property Geek newsletter, as I came across an article headlined "Regulating Airbnb - MP claims cross-party backing for the clampdown". The article describes how a particular Labour MP is looking to make an amendment to the Levelling Up and Regeneration Bill in the House of Commons. This will give English local authorities the power to limit the number of short-term lets through similar planning restrictions we have already seen in London and Scotland. If you take to the comments of the article, it's clear that these restrictions, as all do, face scrutiny. Landlords argue that the introduction of Section 24 is a core reason for the increase in short-term lets, due to the tax advantages discussed earlier. If this is correct, the Government has two options; alleviate Section 24, reduce their tax income, and incentivize landlords to utilise standard tenancy methods once again or, increase taxation on Holiday Lets to make it equally as painful to own property using either strategy, increasing their tax income in the process. Quote me on this - I'm willing to run down my estate road in nothing but budgie smugglers and a cowboy hat if the former comes to fruition.

These restrictions, and potential future restrictions, introduced by local governments are designed to restrict the supply arrow in figure 5, creating a bottleneck for both new and existing short-term accommodation properties. The quantity of restrictions imposed by local planning authorities is increasing, and I believe in the next 2-5 years similar restrictions will be rolled out in both smaller UK cities and coastal locations with particularly high levels of short-term accommodation housing stock. I foresee this being implied using the methodology of a similar "90-day rule" to London or using an Article 4-like directory, which restricted the introduction of new houses of multiple occupation (HMOs) within a certain area of a city boundary without planning permission. We can see the bottleneck restrictions applied to the supply at the present day, but I would now ask the question:

In future, what could governments do to accelerate supply relief?

Going back to my "perfect storm" analogy, the next logical step would be to reduce the incentive to set up holiday lets in the first place. To achieve this, either the demand or the financial incentive to operate short-term accommodation needs to be reduced. For me, this could be easily achieved by removing the Section 24 tax advantages that holiday let operators currently achieve. In the process of relieving the problems described earlier, the government would increase their tax revenue. At a very high level then, the government could alleviate this issue by hitting two birds with one stone. Alternatively, the demand for short term accommodation would need to be reduced to achieve a similar reduction in supply. From a cynical perspective, if and when the current international travel burdens alleviate and travel returns to what most consider normal, you don't have to connect too many dots to conclude that demand for UK-based short-term accommodation will decrease, at least in terms of holidayers in the market. Another point, which I have tried to avoid as much as possible in this book, is that we are currently in a time where the central banks of the world are tightening monetary policy at an alarming rate. On 3rd of November 2022, the Bank of England raised interest rates to 3%, and I personally believe that throughout early 2023 we will see further tightening as inflation remains rampant. As of the time of writing, the unemployment rate remains low, although this is a lagging indicator of tightening monetary policy. I will be keeping a keen eye on unemployment rates as I think that will directly influence demand for short-term accommodation. Do remember, going on holidays and taking breaks are not essential for families who are seeing a loss of real household income, therefore I believe that the tighter the economy gets, the less demand for short-term accommodation will be present. If your properties are offering contractors a cost-effective, short-term, housing option and it's located in the vicinity of jobs and the fundamentals, then you stand the best chance of maintaining strong demand, although even this may be at risk if job losses start to rise. You may think COVID has changed the holiday market permanently, which I personally don't, but if you do you may consider that demand will continue at a high level indefinitely. If you want to protect yourself against a reduction in demand, look to acquire R2RSA properties within locations which aren't currently saturated with short-term accommodation properties, as discussed earlier in this book.

I appreciate I have thrown a lot of statistics at you over the past few paragraphs, so let me do a full circle and bring us back to the purpose of this chapter. What is the future of R2RSA? Here are my thoughts, take them or leave them. Brace yourself, they are quite bold, but I'd more than welcome thoughts on the contrary.

Time Frame: 1 - 2 years

Prediction: The supply of short-term accommodation increases. Demand stays somewhat level, but the supply continues to increase nationwide where restrictions have not been brought into force and therefore occupancy rates start to decrease per operator. Operators primarily effected by the reduction of occupancy will be those in less desirable areas with a less diversified customer base. Unless the current rise in rental demand begins to reverse, landlords will continue to raise rent, therefore profitability will be squeezed for Rent to Rent operators unless demand remains high and the market accepts higher nightly rates. Supply restrictions in the form of planning applications will continue to roll out nationwide. Large R2RSA companies will continue building their portfolios. Some companies will de-risk by starting to adopt other strategies and purchase properties rather than rent them, others will continue to acquire R2RSA properties building highly profitable portfolios with high rental exposure.

Time Frame: 2 - 5 years

Prediction: 90-day rule style restrictions for short-term properties are now nationwide, drastically cooling the growth curve but not reducing the supply of short-term let properties. Less serious R2RSA operators will leave the market as they don't have the appetite to negotiate with planning control measures. The poor quality sourcers will move onto other unregulated markets to cause havoc without restriction. Even quality sourcers will be squeezed as they now need to source properties owned by a landlord who:

- Accepts short-term accommodation in their property through a company
- Owns a property that is financially and legally suitable for R2RSA (which is already difficult)

- Is willing to wait 4 - 8 weeks, untenanted, with no income, whilst an application to the local authority goes through, which may be rejected anyway.

This will make sourcing next to impossible. Only existing serious operators remain in the market, but restrictions coming into force for existing properties put their portfolios at risk of being rationalised. I believe the demand will have cooled down due to international travel restrictions being alleviated and the macroeconomy will be either in or just exiting a recession, but the supply will have been steadily rising, causing occupancy rates to decrease further. Those companies who didn't de-risk, liable for hundreds of thousands of pounds of rent, per month, will likely find they are over-leveraged and will sign off break clauses left right and centre.

Time Frame: 5 years +

Prediction: The strategy remains lucrative but only serious hosts remain. Those who remain will be the excellent hosts who have primarily focused on meeting local laws, treating landlords well and creating an excellent service for their guests. I hope that you will fall within this category if you follow the principles outlined in this book. The strategy will be kept buoyant in heavily populated areas as contractors still take advantage of cost-effective accommodation. Very few new individuals will pick the strategy up because sourcers will be rare and planning restrictions will be too big of a barrier. Holiday lets will remain, as the flexibility of owning the properties allows the owners to apply for licences whilst receiving income from longer-term tenants. Although, the supply of Holiday Lets will be slowed due to the restrictions implied by the Government.

If these predictions are wrong, I'll be the first to hold my hands up, but the above concludes my interpretation of the future market based on the facts I see today. Legal restrictions associated with short term accommodation in the United Kingdom are coming, where the window to set R2RSA properties up and secure sourcing fee's is closing. My recommendation is then, if you are looking to secure additional income using the strategy, using any of the income generation methods described in Chapter 3, the time is now. The route to entry is about to get harder, But I'll illiterate again, please run your business in a responsible way, as I have outlined within the earlier chapters, through respectful operation and risk aversion techniques.

As a final comment from me then, I will share how I plan to proceed with my R2RSA portfolio in this upcoming marketplace. I plan to continue acquiring R2RSA properties, but with a *"proceed with caution"* approach. Bear in mind that even utilising the R2RSA strategy at all is not particularly cautious as it's littered with risk and exposes you to a substantial amount of rental demand, so I would interpret that you are probably not the most cautious individual if you're deploying this strategy at all. However, there are profits to be made, and I plan to take advantage but not expose myself to enough risk that it could bankrupt me should the short-term market turn aggressively negative. What this means then, is through my other forms of income, I want to be able to afford the rental payments without turning negative while my properties perform at 30% occupancy. I concluded the 30% figure as I rarely have seen any well-positioned property with strong fundamentals regularly achieve less occupancy than this. I then calculate the loss I would incur at 30% occupancy per property and sum the number of properties I have until it matches that of my disposable income after paying all my essential living costs. I will show you a theoretical example.

Let's say post living costs I have £1750 per calendar month as disposable income from non-property related income streams of which I would normally invest or save. Here are some theoretical losses of various properties at 30% occupancy levels.

Property 1: - £256pcm @ 30% occupancy

Property 2: - £421pcm @ 30% occupancy

Property 3: - £398pcm @ 30% occupancy

Property 4: - £645pcm @ 30% occupancy

Property 5: - £197pcm @ 30% occupancy

Property 6: - £385pcm @ 30% occupancy

The sum loss of these properties would be £2302pcm. This would be over my disposable income per month and could lead to bankruptcy if I had no cash reserve. However, if I removed Property 4, then my losses would be a maximum of £1657pcm. In this case, even if all of the properties performed at 30% occupancy, which in my opinion is highly unlikely, I still would not turn negative. Note that to choose which property you remove, you wouldn't simply look at losses at 30% occupancy, you would look at profitability, set-up costs, location, average occupancy rate and far more described in this book to determine the best and worst performing properties. The above is simply for demonstration purposes. When I have demonstrated my protective methods described above to genuine property investors, and by genuine, I mean those who purchase properties rather than rent them, most have concluded that even my more conservative view is back sh*t crazy. At face value, preparing to lose that sum of money monthly does sound outrageous. But do bear in mind, at the typical 70% occupancy rate of which we expect our well-positioned portfolio to perform, these properties may well positively cash flow a multiplier of 2 to 3 times those loss projections. It's about looking at the probable worst-case scenario, protecting yourself, and then operating the business under an educated risk. If I had less disposable income, I would take on fewer properties, if I had more disposable income, I would potentially take on more. This is just a rule of thumb I use to protect myself from a complete personal financial breakdown. If you want to inherit more risk and completely over-leverage yourself with rental demand compared to that of your income, that's your provocative.

If you want to take it even further and give up your current income completely and have your mortgage, living standards, family and car hanging in the balance of this high-risk strategy, then again, that is your provocative, but it's an approach I certainly would avoid.

You could use the other income Methods 2 or 3 (See Chapter 3) to increase your income streams which are risk-free in terms of payment liability. The beauty of R2RSA is that you have the choice to pursue whichever strategies you want. Whatever you decide to do, I hope this book was somewhat useful in helping you decide whether this strategy is right for you.

Conclusion

I imagine you have purchased this book to investigate a strategy which can allow you to earn additional income. Therefore, as I conclude, I want to pull together the financial income streams I have discussed throughout this book to demonstrate the income possibilities through this strategy. I have done my best to use realistic figures based on real life experience, and present realistic targets to achieve in the time frame of 12 months, but please understand that these numbers are theoretical and by no means should be taken as a certainty when entering the space. Please also understand that you need to accept the risks associated with each income method described in this book if you wish to profit from them.

With the goal of acquiring six average R2RSA properties within your portfolio and self-managing each of them, we calculated that Income Method 1, operating your own R2RSA properties, within the example would generate £3362.40pcm, or £40348.80 annually (post corporation tax, assuming all profit i.e. ignoring set up costs). Of course, to achieve this you would either require the set-up capital immediately to fund acquisition or you could re-invest profits into acquiring subsequent properties, although this will likely extend your timeframe beyond 12 months.

With the goal of managing five average R2RSA properties on behalf of other investors, we calculated that Income Method 2, managing R2RSA properties, within the example would generate £1017.00pcm, or £12,204 annually (post corporation tax).

With the goal of sourcing and selling two properties per month to investors, we calculated that Income Method 3, sourcing R2RSA properties for investors, within the example would generate £4125.00pcm, or £49,500 annually (post corporation tax).

To summarise then, if you were in a position to operate your R2RSA business under the Strategy Recommendation, Scenario 4 – Time Rich with Disposable Capital and could achieve the results described above, we have calculated a total income generation of £102,053 per annum, or £8504.40pcm, under the very specific conditions of the examples provided in this book. In reality, you may be operating under any combination of the income methods and strategy recommendations. For someone like myself using this strategy as an income supplement, you may only set up one or two properties and source on the side, reducing your income considerably compared to the above example, however reducing your risk in parallel. Obviously, your company's income is completely fluid based on performance and risk tolerance, but I hope this summary at least provides an idea of how the diversified income methods interlink together, creating an R2RSA business.

As part of my final comments, I want to very briefly re-enforce the core messages that I have tried to describe throughout. R2RSA is a vehicle you can use to generate additional income. I have described what the income streams are in Chapter 3, so use this as a guide to determine which best suits you, if any, based on your time and capital restrictions. Using Chapter 4, understand the risks of each Method and conclude if you are comfortable operating under these risks. Using Chapter 5, you can set up your business ready to deploy your chosen method in full compliance with the law. I have described in Chapters 6 & 7 how to deploy your chosen method. If you are planning on sourcing R2RSA properties, please do not present investors with investments which do not pass the statutory checks described. Do not withhold sourcing fees from investors should an investment fall through. If you are setting up your own properties, perform full financial checks to accurately predict the set up and ongoing costs of operation. Pay landlords in full and on time for the agreed rent. Frankly, we should be thanking our lucky stars that landlords even consider company lets after the past 3 years+ of abuse from less considerate serviced accommodation operators. Pay for damage of which your guests cause. Take out appropriate insurances if you want to cover contents and damage. If you're looking to manage R2RSA properties for other businesses, ensure that you utilise the suite of online tools to maximise profitability for all stakeholders. Now you know how to run your R2RSA business properly, and you know what pitfalls to avoid on your journey, you are in a great position to find further education and/or start generating addition income using the strategy. As we have seen in Chapter 8, the window will slowly close over the medium term, so the opportunity to take advantage of this lucrative strategy is closing. However, I wouldn't recommend rushing into setting up a business tomorrow. Perform any further due diligence you require and then start to take action when/if you feel ready. The initial feedback I received from those who have read a draft of this book have suggested that I haven't really "sold" the strategy. I appreciate that in some cases what I have highlighted could be interpreted as negative towards the strategy. However, the purpose of writing this book was to give an honest review. The issues I have highlighted in the book aren't commonly shared with those who are entering the industry. With this said, I believe R2RSA is the highest returning strategy in the property sector. As you have seen throughout the book, we see returns of 100% or 200% on your invested capital when operating R2RSA properties, a figure completely out of the reach of B2L or HMO strategies. This is not theory; I have personally experienced it. The fact that I have highlighted common pitfalls should not put you off getting involved, as I believe I have provided methods to mitigate against these. Knowing this information will save you thousands in losses due to making the common mistakes. I will stress again that you are in a much better position than I was when I started my R2RSA journey, and I like to think I have made it work, therefore so can you.

At the start of this book, I also mentioned that I would recommend trusted training providers if you wished to take your education further and get one to one support whilst building your portfolio. Despite the upfront cost, as with any mentorship, it's necessary to understand that having supporting mentors will fast track your performance and also maintain your accountability. I can guarantee that curve balls will raise their heads of which I won't have directly addressed throughout this book. Do bear in mind, I have personally paid for tuition fees and would suggest that any profits I have made thus far would not have been possible without training. I actually consider the training free, as the R2RSA properties I sourced and sold onto investors have more than paid for training costs, and my business continues to make monthly profits on top of that from the properties I am operating. Therefore, although training comes at a cost, I consider it an investment of which is now providing returns. Part of me feels like training is a service I could provide, but unfortunately, outside of generic advise, I am no trainer. I frankly don't have the patience, so it's not something I plan on, or wish to, pursue indefinitely. However, do feel free to get in contact using my email address below, let me know which of the *"Strategy Recommendations"* from Chapter 3 is most applicable to you, and I will make my wholehearted training recommendation if this is the route you wish to pursue. In addition, I also promised that I would recommend reliable R2RSA sourcers and management companies should you wish to use a similar strategy to myself, described as Scenario 2 in Chapter 3. Again, do feel free to contact me via email and I am happy to provide you with a recommendation. This will help you avoid any of the sourcing scams and/or poor management associated with some of the businesses in the industry.

I have tried to keep this book as concise as possible, but if you feel you need more information, feel free to get in contact and I will do my best to help where I can. The free end of book resources I would like to share include:

- Financial Analysis Spreadsheet
- Agent/Contact Log
- Property Furniture List
- Example Company Let Contract
- Example Management Contract
- Example Non-Disclosure Agreement
- Links to Helpful Resources

This is where I will get a bit cheeky and ask for a couple of minutes of your time. I would really appreciate a quick book review on the Amazon E-Book website. If you have bought a PDF copy of the book, instead of an Amazon review, I would again appreciate a Facebook review for the book on my company Facebook page www.facebook.com/studleyproperties/. I know it's a pain, but it would help me improve my future work and get the book out to more of those looking to enter the industry. I would love to hear from you, so send a screenshot of your published review to my email frank.roberts@studleyproperties.co.uk and I will aim to respond with your free resources as quickly as possible!

Other than that, good luck with your future endeavours and take care of yourself.

- *Frank Roberts*

Printed in Great Britain
by Amazon